REDUCING INEQUALITIES

Between Lesbian, Gay, Bisexual, Transgender, and Queer Adolescents and Cisgender, Heterosexual Adolescents

PROCEEDINGS OF A WORKSHOP

Erin Hammers Forstag, *Rapporteur*

Board on Children, Youth, and Families

Division of Behavioral and Social Sciences and Education

The National Academies of
SCIENCES · ENGINEERING · MEDICINE

THE NATIONAL ACADEMIES PRESS
Washington, DC
www.nap.edu

THE NATIONAL ACADEMIES PRESS   500 Fifth Street, NW   Washington, DC 20001

This activity was supported by a contract between the National Academy of Sciences and William T. Grant Foundation (189982), and the National Academy of Sciences President's Committee (unnumbered). Additional support was provided by the National Academy of Sciences W. K. Kellogg Foundation Fund. Any opinions, findings, conclusions, or recommendations expressed in this publication do not necessarily reflect the views of any organization or agency that provided support for the project.

International Standard Book Number-13: 978-0-309-27298-8
International Standard Book Number-10: 0-309-27298-X
Digital Object Identifier: https://doi.org/10.17226/26383

Additional copies of this publication are available from the National Academies Press, 500 Fifth Street, NW, Keck 360, Washington, DC 20001; (800) 624-6242 or (202) 334-3313; http://www.nap.edu.

Copyright 2022 by the National Academy of Sciences. All rights reserved.

Printed in the United States of America

Suggested citation: National Academies of Sciences, Engineering, and Medicine. (2022). *Reducing Inequalities Between LGBTQ Adolescents and Cisgender, Heterosexual Adolescents: Proceedings of a Workshop*. Washington, DC: The National Academies Press. https://doi.org/10.17226/26383.

The National Academies of
SCIENCES · ENGINEERING · MEDICINE

The **National Academy of Sciences** was established in 1863 by an Act of Congress, signed by President Lincoln, as a private, nongovernmental institution to advise the nation on issues related to science and technology. Members are elected by their peers for outstanding contributions to research. Dr. Marcia McNutt is president.

The **National Academy of Engineering** was established in 1964 under the charter of the National Academy of Sciences to bring the practices of engineering to advising the nation. Members are elected by their peers for extraordinary contributions to engineering. Dr. John L. Anderson is president.

The **National Academy of Medicine** (formerly the Institute of Medicine) was established in 1970 under the charter of the National Academy of Sciences to advise the nation on medical and health issues. Members are elected by their peers for distinguished contributions to medicine and health. Dr. Victor J. Dzau is president.

The three Academies work together as the **National Academies of Sciences, Engineering, and Medicine** to provide independent, objective analysis and advice to the nation and conduct other activities to solve complex problems and inform public policy decisions. The National Academies also encourage education and research, recognize outstanding contributions to knowledge, and increase public understanding in matters of science, engineering, and medicine.

Learn more about the National Academies of Sciences, Engineering, and Medicine at **www.nationalacademies.org**.

The National Academies of
SCIENCES • ENGINEERING • MEDICINE

Consensus Study Reports published by the National Academies of Sciences, Engineering, and Medicine document the evidence-based consensus on the study's statement of task by an authoring committee of experts. Reports typically include findings, conclusions, and recommendations based on information gathered by the committee and the committee's deliberations. Each report has been subjected to a rigorous and independent peer-review process and it represents the position of the National Academies on the statement of task.

Proceedings published by the National Academies of Sciences, Engineering, and Medicine chronicle the presentations and discussions at a workshop, symposium, or other event convened by the National Academies. The statements and opinions contained in proceedings are those of the participants and are not endorsed by other participants, the planning committee, or the National Academies.

For information about other products and activities of the National Academies, please visit www.nationalacademies.org/about/whatwedo.

PLANNING COMMITTEE ON REDUCING INEQUALITIES BETWEEN LGBTQ ADOLESCENTS AND CISGENDER, HETEROSEXUAL ADOLESCENTS: A WORKSHOP

STEPHEN T. RUSSELL (*Chair*), University of Texas, Austin
AISHA CANFIELD-ALLEN, Ceres Policy Research
DAVID CHAE, Tulane University
NAT DURAN, Illinois Safe Schools Alliance
ERROL L. FIELDS, Johns Hopkins School of Medicine
JESSICA N. FISH, University of Maryland
AMORIE ROBINSON, Ruth Ellis Center
JAMA SHELTON, Hunter College

Staff

AMANDA GRIGG, *Program Officer*
MARISSA GLOVER, *Senior Program Assistant*
NATACHA BLAIN, *Board Director*
EMILY BACKES, *Senior Program Officer*

BOARD ON CHILDREN, YOUTH, AND FAMILIES

DAVID V.B. BRITT (*Chair*), Retired, Sesame Workshop
HAROLYN BELCHER, Center for Diversity in Public Health Leadership Training, Kennedy Krieger Institute, Professor of Pediatrics, Johns Hopkins University School of Medicine
RICHARD F. CATALANO, School of Social Work, University of Washington, Co-founder, Social Development Research Group
TAMMY CHANG, Department of Family Medicine, University of Michigan
DIMITRI CHRISTAKIS, Center for Child Health, Behavior, and Development, Seattle Children's Research Institute, University of Washington
GREG DUNCAN, School of Education, University of California, Irvine
NANCY E. HILL, Harvard University, Graduate School of Education
STEPHANIE J. MONROE, President, The Wrenwood Group, LLC
JAMES M. PERRIN, Harvard Medical School, MassGeneral Hospital for Children
NISHA SACHDEV, Center for Health and Health Care in Schools, George Washington University Milken Institute of Public Health
MARTIN H. TEICHER, Developmental Biopsychiatry Research Program, McLean, Harvard Medical School
JONATHAN TODRES, Georgia State University College of Law
JOANNA LEE WILLIAMS, Rutgers University, Graduate School of Applied and Professional Psychology

NATACHA BLAIN, *Director*

Acknowledgments

This Proceedings of a Workshop was reviewed in draft form by individuals chosen for their diverse perspectives and technical expertise. The purpose of this independent review is to provide candid and critical comments that will assist the National Academies of Sciences, Engineering, and Medicine in making each published proceedings as sound as possible and to ensure that it meets the institutional standards for quality, objectivity, evidence, and responsiveness to the charge. The review comments and draft manuscript remain confidential to protect the integrity of the process.

We thank the following individuals for their review of these proceedings: Jessica N. Fish, Department of Family Science, School of Public Health, University of Maryland. We also thank staff member Tom Arrison for reading and providing helpful comments on the manuscript. Although the reviewers provided many constructive comments and suggestions, they were not asked to endorse the content of the proceedings nor did they see the final draft before its release.

The review of these proceedings was overseen by Karina L. Walters, School of Social Work, University of Washington. She was responsible for making certain that an independent examination of these proceedings was carried out in accordance with standards of the National Academies and that all review comments were carefully considered. Responsibility for the final content rests entirely with the rapporteur and the National Academies.

Preface

We are pleased to introduce these proceedings of the National Academies of Sciences, Engineering, and Medicine workshop on Reducing Inequalities Between LGBTQ Adolescents and Cisgender, Heterosexual Adolescents. The broadest goal of the workshop was to explore effective programs, policies, and practices for reducing inequalities in the areas of mental, emotional, behavioral, and physical health of U.S. lesbian, gay, bisexual, transgender, and queer (LGBTQ) youth ages 13–25.[1] The workshop addressed the interpersonal, institutional, and structural factors associated with the inequities that exist and are widening for LGBTQ youth compared to cisgender, heterosexual youth. In particular, the planning committee made a commitment to focus on the experiences of LGBTQ youth of color, strategies for supporting them, and lessons to be learned from their experiences.

The workshop was informed by prior work at the National Academies, including two important recent consensus studies: *The Promise of Adolescence: Realizing Opportunity for All Youth* (2019), and *Understanding the Well-Being of LGBTQI+ Populations* (2020). *The Promise of Adolescence* explores the neurobiological and social-behavioral processes that characterize the developmental period, and that lay the foundation for trajectories for the rest of the life course. The report synthesized the dramatic advances

---

[1] A recent study (National Academies of Sciences, Engineering, and Medicine, 2019) refers to the period of adolescence as encompassing four periods, from early adolescence to young adulthood. The focus of this workshop will be on middle adolescence (starting at age 13) through young adulthood (ages 19–25). The term "youth" in these proceedings encompasses adolescents ages 13–25.

in understandings of adolescent brain development and plasticity, and the dynamics between that development and the physical, psychological, interpersonal, social, institutional, and cultural influences that shape adolescents' lives. A key focus was on inequity, including substantial attention to the lives and well-being of LGBTQ adolescents.[2] The report illuminates the promise and possibility of development during the adolescent years, and focuses on the implications for social systems that shape adolescence—their families and communities, systems of care, schools, and health.

One year later, *Understanding the Status and Well-Being of Sexual and Gender Diverse Populations* assessed the state of knowledge about the status and well-being of sexual- and gender-diverse people. The report was the first by the National Academies to take a truly broad approach to understanding well-being—extending beyond physical and mental health[3] to include family and community well-being, as well as the cultural, legal, educational, economic, and religious institutions that shape the lives and well-being of sexual- and gender-diverse people.

Our workshop built on the foundations in those National Academies reports, with the goal of examining inequalities in mental, emotional, behavioral, and physical health among LGBTQ youth, what is known about strategies for supporting them, lessons to be learned from these strategies, and how to reduce inequities through programs, practices, and policies. The planning committee sought expertise from researchers to summarize the state of the evidence, although the committee was aware that efforts focused on actually reducing inequality (rather than simply measuring it) have rarely been empirically tested. The committee was particularly motivated to seek input from professionals and practitioners whose daily and lived experience is in the service of LGBTQ adolescents, and to hear from LGBTQ youth of color about their perspectives, lives, and recommendations.

We are grateful to the extraordinary planning committee, composed of experts in fields of research, practice, and policy in the service of LGBTQ youth. Through their vision and networks, we assembled an amazing group of workshop sessions and speakers, focusing first on key concepts and definitions, research on what is known about reducing inequalities through prevention and intervention, and perspectives from youths. We then focused on four domains or contexts that shape the lives of LGBTQ youth: their families and communities; systems of care, including child welfare and carceral systems; education; and health. For each domain we invited experts

---

[2] A recent report (Akhmadikina, Saba, and Russell, 2021) reviews inclusion of LGBTQ youth in *The Promise of Adolescence*.

[3] A prior report (Institute of Medicine, 2011) was transformational in the field of physical and mental health science and policy.

in research to synthesize existing evidence, followed by panel discussions that included researchers, practitioners, and policy advocates working with LGBTQ youth in each of those domains. Across all sessions and panels, we asked all participants to keep the following principles in mind:

- That the focus be on solutions or reductions in equality that can impact the long-term well-being of LGBTQ youth;
- That the domains we highlight are intertwined and cannot be understood in isolation;
- That youth and their experiences are intersectional in terms of race, ethnicity, cultural and religious background, and other identities, including intersex youth, youth with differences in sexual development, and youth who are not out; and
- That while we are compelled to focus on vulnerabilities and inequalities, most LGBTQ youth thrive and contribute to their own well-being and to their communities.

We acknowledged the ever-evolving language of LGBTQ, recognizing the importance, meaning, and limitations of language, as well as the ways that our words and labels may shape both the way youth see and feel about themselves as well as public opinion about them. We further acknowledged the urgent need to center the experiences of Black, Brown, and Indigenous people of color, while acknowledging that naming may not resonate with all youth who are marginalized or minoritized. Ultimately, we acknowledged the goal of affirming language that can recognize the multidimensional nature of identity.

During the period of three half-days on August 25, 26, and 27, 2021, the workshop was conducted virtually, and reached over 600 participants. Although originally intended to be held in person, the experience illuminated the significant interest and motivation by people from across the U.S. and around the world to learn from the workshop program and engage with the goals of reducing inequalities for LGBTQ adolescents.

These proceedings illuminate the rich and growing body of evidence on the lives and well-being of LGBTQ adolescents, but also point to the limits of existing evidence for truly identifying the programs, practices, and policies that may reduce inequalities, particularly for LGBTQ youth of color. Yet the perspectives of the practice, policy, and youth experts pointed to promising strategies that are clearly making a difference in communities and for youth every day. Illuminating these strategies was the fundamental goal of the workshop and, in doing so, we hope to have sparked the next generation of research, practice, and policy that will support the well-being of LGBTQ adolescents, particularly LGBTQ youth of color.

Finally, we are grateful to the William T. Grant Foundation and the

National Academies W.K. Kellogg Foundation Fund for the funding to make the workshop possible. Our hope is that this workshop will stimulate further interest in understanding the evidence base for reducing inequality among LGBTQ adolescents, including studies that could further explore the evidence base in depth and provide clear and actionable recommendations for researchers, practitioners, educators, policy makers, youth, and their families.

> Stephen T. Russell, *Chair*
> Planning Committee on Reducing Inequalities
> Between LGBTQ Adolescents and Cisgender,
> Heterosexual Adolescents

REFERENCES

Akhmadikina, N., Saba, V., and Russell, S.T. 2021. *The Promise of Adolescence: Highlighting the Experiences of LGBTQ Youth*. The Stories and Numbers Project. Available: https://storiesandnumbers.org/wp-content/uploads/2021/09/The-Promise-of-Adolescence-Brief.pdf.

Institute of Medicine of the National Academies. 2011. *The Health of Lesbian, Gay, Bisexual, and Transgender People: Building a Foundation for Better Understanding*. Washington, DC: The National Academies Press. Available: https://www.ncbi.nlm.nih.gov/books/NBK64806/.

National Academies of Sciences, Engineering, and Medicine. 2019. *The Promise of Adolescence: Realizing Opportunity for All Youth*. Washington, DC: The National Academies Press. Available: https://doi.org/10.17226/25388.

National Academies of Sciences, Engineering, and Medicine. 2020. *Understanding the Well-Being of LGBTQI+ Populations*. Washington, DC: The National Academies Press. Available: https://doi.org/10.17226/25877.

Contents

1   INTRODUCTION   1
Background, 1
Organization of the Proceedings, 2
Opening Remarks, 2
Key Concepts and Definitions, 4
Research Landscape, 5
Policy Landscape, 8
Reflections, 11

2   LGBTQ YOUTH OF COLOR   13
Lived Expertise, 13
    How Do You Define Health and Well-Being?, 14
    What Are Promising Solutions to Inequalities in Health and Well-Being That You Have Seen Work in Your Community?, 14
    What Are the Barriers to These Types of Solutions?, 14
    Who Are the Influential People in Your Community and How Can We Support Them?, 15
    If You Had a Magic Wand, What System Would You Change and How?, 15
    What Are Common Misconceptions About Youth?, 16
    How Does Your Racial or Ethnic Identity Shape the Way You Experience Your Sexual Orientation and/or Gender Identity?, 16

How Do You Think COVID-19 Has Impacted LGBTQ
  Young People and the Community as a Whole?, 17
Research Landscape, 18
Exploring Racism and Sexual Identity During the COVID-19
  Pandemic, 20
Systems of Support, 21
Reflections, 22

3 PROMISING INTERVENTIONS IN PERSONAL, CARCERAL,
  AND CARE SYSTEMS   27
  Landscape: Outcomes, Inequalities, and Known Interventions, 27
  Paths Forward in Research, 28
  Promising Interventions, 30
    Juvenile Carceral System Intervention: Youth Justice
      Agency Policies and Professional Development, 30
    Child Welfare System Intervention: The American Civil
      Liberties Union of Illinois and the Illinois Department
      of Children and Family Services, 32
    Child Welfare System Intervention: National Quality
      Improvement Center, 35
  Reflections, 37

4 PROMISING INTERVENTIONS FOR FAMILIES AND
  COMMUNITIES   39
  Research Landscape: Outcomes and Known Interventions, 39
  Promising Interventions, 40
    Family Interventions: Lead with Love and PATHS, 40
    Community Intervention: Community Centers and
      CenterLink, 43
    Community Intervention: Rainbow Pride Youth
      Alliance, 45
  Reflections, 47

5 PROMISING INTERVENTIONS IN MENTAL, EMOTIONAL,
  AND PHYSICAL HEALTH   49
  Landscape: Outcomes, Inequalities, and Known Interventions, 49
  Promising Interventions, 50
    Mental Health Intervention: EQuIP, 51
    Mental Health Intervention: AFFIRM, 53
    Mental Health Interventions: The Trevor Project, 54
    Physical Health Intervention: HIV Prevention, 56
  Reflections, 58

6	**PROMISING INTERVENTIONS IN EDUCATION**
	Landscape: Outcomes, Inequalities, and Known Interventions, 61
	Promising Interventions, 65
	    School-Based Intervention: Broward County Public
	        Schools' LGBTQ+ Coordinator, 65
	    School-Based Intervention: Comprehensive Sex
	        Education, 66
	    School-Based Intervention: GSA Clubs, 68
	Reflections, 69
		61

7	**CLOSING REFLECTIONS**	71
	REFERENCES	73
	APPENDIXES	
A	Workshop Agenda	83
B	Biographical Sketches of Planning Committee Members and Workshop Speakers	87

Acronyms and Abbreviations

BIPOC	Black, Indigenous, people of color
CBPR	Community-based, participatory research
CBT	Cognitive behavioral therapy
CSE	Comprehensive sexual education
EQuIP	Empowering Queer Identities in Psychotherapy
GSA	Clubs formerly known as Gay-Straight Alliances; now referred to either as Genders & Sexualities Alliances or simply GSAs.
LGB	Lesbian, gay, and bisexual
LGBT	Lesbian, gay, bisexual, and transgender
LGBTQ	Lesbian, gay, bisexual, transgender, and queer/questioning
LGBTQ+	Lesbian, gay, bisexual, transgender, queer/questioning, and others
LGBTQ2S	Lesbian, gay, bisexual, transgender, queer/questioning, and two spirit
LGBTQI	Lesbian, gay, bisexual, transgender, queer/questioning, and intersex
MEB	Mental, emotional, behavioral
MSM	Men who have sex with men

PATHS	Parents and Adolescents Talking about Healthy Sexuality
PUSH	Providing Unique Support for Health
RCT	Randomized controlled trial
RPYA	Rainbow Pride Youth Alliance
SGD	Sexual- and gender-diverse
SGM	Sexual and gender minority
SIECUS	Sexuality Information and Education Council of the U.S.
SOGIE	Sexual orientation and gender identity and expression
STI	Sexually transmitted infection

1

Introduction

BACKGROUND

To better understand the inequalities facing lesbian, gay, bisexual, transgender, and queer (LGBTQ) youth and the promising interventions being used to address these inequalities, the National Academies of Sciences, Engineering, and Medicine's Board on Children, Youth, and Families hosted a virtual public workshop titled Reducing Inequalities Between LGBTQ Adolescents and Cisgender, Heterosexual Adolescents, which convened on August 25–27, 2021. The workshop was developed by a planning committee composed of experts from the fields of sociology, medicine, public health, psychology, social work, policy, and direct-service provision. This Proceedings of a Workshop summarizes the presentations and discussions from that workshop.

On day one of the workshop, speakers explored key concepts and frameworks necessary to understand inequalities facing LGBTQ youth and reviewed the policy and research landscapes around LGBTQ youth well-being (see Appendix A for complete agenda). Exploring interventions that address differences among sexual-minority youth across the intersecting social identities of race, ethnicity, cultural background, gender, and gender identity was a primary aim of the workshop. Day one concluded with a panel highlighting the lived experience of LGBTQ youth of color and a panel focused on the state of knowledge regarding outcomes and interventions for LGBTQ youth of color. Speakers on workshop days two and three detailed promising interventions being used to reduce inequalities in the domains of health, education, family, and community, as well as in systems of care and juvenile justice.

ORGANIZATION OF THE PROCEEDINGS

This proceedings describes the workshop panel presentations and the discussion that followed each panel. The chapters are organized around the key topics of the workshop, with some chapters including summaries of related content from multiple panels. Chapter 1 highlights key concepts and definitions, including an overview of sexual and gender diversity and inequalities. This chapter applies an intersectional lens to LGBTQ youth well-being, and reviews the research and policy landscape. Chapter 2 focuses broadly on outcomes and interventions for LGBTQ youth of color, and includes a summary of the workshop's lived experience panel. Chapters 3 through 6 offer insights into key inequalities facing LGBTQ youth in various domains, and these chapters highlight promising interventions for addressing inequalities in these areas. Chapter 3 focuses on personal, carceral, and care systems; Chapter 4 focuses on family and community; Chapter 5 addresses mental, emotional, and physical health; and Chapter 6 addresses education. Finally, Chapter 7 summarizes reflections shared in the workshop's closing sessions.

The full meeting agenda and biographical sketches of planning committee members and workshop presenters appear in the appendices. A full recording of the workshop and the speakers' presentations have been archived online.[1]

This proceedings has been prepared by the workshop rapporteur as a factual summary of what occurred at the workshop. The views contained in the proceedings are those of the individual workshop participants and do not necessarily represent the views of other workshop participants, the workshop planning committee, or the National Academies.

OPENING REMARKS

Stephen Russell (University of Texas at Austin), chair of the workshop planning committee, welcomed workshop participants and called attention to two reports from the National Academies that are relevant to the topic at hand. In 2019, *The Promise of Adolescence* was published; this consensus report explored how changes in brain structure, function, and connectivity create a period of opportunity and possibility during adolescence (NASEM, 2019). Russell noted that, for the purposes of this workshop, the planning committee adopted the definition of adolescence from the 2019 report. Rather than a specific age range, adolescence is a period of complex social changes that begin in late childhood and last through multiple social transitions into adulthood, he said. In 2020, the National Academies published

---

[1] For more information, see: https://www.nationalacademies.org/event/08-25-2021/reducing-inequalities-between-lgbtq-adolescents-and-cisgender-heterosexual-adolescents-a-workshop.

Understanding the Well-Being of LGBTQI+ Populations, which was motivated by the growing prevalence and visibility of sexual- and gender-diverse (SGD) people in the U.S. and around the world, and the need for greater understanding of the ways that laws, systems, and programs affect their well-being (NASEM, 2020).

Over the last decade, said Russell, it has become evident that disparities related to sexual orientation and gender identity are going in the wrong direction, particularly for subgroups of SGD youth, such as youth of color and youth with plurisexual identities. These same subgroups have historically been excluded from research on LGBTQ youth, meaning that the most marginalized and disadvantaged populations are also the least understood. The present workshop, said Russell, aims to explore three questions posed in the Statement of Task (see Box 1-1).

The planning committee set several priorities for the workshop. First, the committee prioritized inviting speakers with diverse experiences in terms of identities, disciplines, and institutions, and also included the perspectives of young people themselves. Second, the workshop was designed to focus on solutions and promising interventions, rather than on simply identifying known inequalities in the well-being of LGBTQ youth. Third,

---

BOX 1-1
Statement of Task

A planning committee appointed by the National Academies of Sciences, Engineering, and Medicine will plan and execute a virtual 2-day public workshop focused on examining inequalities in mental, emotional, behavioral (MEB), and physical health among LGBTQ youth, what is known about strategies for supporting them, lessons to be learned from these strategies, and how to reduce inequities through programs, practices, and policies. The workshop will focus on the following questions:

1. What is the current evidence on MEB and physical health outcomes among LGBTQ youth, in particular LGBTQ youth of color, and what is known about the relationship between these outcomes on academic performance, later MEB and physical health, and future educational and career success?
2. What is known about the role of interpersonal factors, such as the development of peer, romantic, and sexual relationships, social support, and social isolation, in relation to MEB and physical health outcomes among LGBTQ youth, in particular LGBTQ youth of color?
3. What practices, programs, and policies have shown promise in supporting the MEB and physical health of LGBTQ youth, in particular LGBTQ youth of color?

the committee asked speakers to recognize connections between areas of inequality; Russell noted that systems such as education, juvenile justice, and child welfare are intertwined. Finally, said Russell, it is critical to acknowledge the diversity of identities among LGBTQ young people, and to recognize that experiences may differ dramatically from person to person. Relatedly, he said, the language used to refer to these communities is ever evolving and does not always capture the diverse understanding that young people have of who they are. Russell said that the committee aimed for the use of affirming language that recognizes the multidimensional nature of identity, and that he looked forward to learning from workshop speakers about how to do this better.

KEY CONCEPTS AND DEFINITIONS

To introduce and frame the topics of the workshop, the first panel described the current state of sexual and gender diversity in the U.S., and gave an overview of the research and policy landscape in this area. Russell Toomey (University of Arizona) began by noting that sexual- and gender-diverse (SGD) youth are aware of and disclosing their identities at younger ages than did prior generations. For example, the Generations Study[2] found that the youngest cohort were aware of their same-sex attractions at age 11, compared to age 13 for the oldest cohort (Bishop et al., 2020). The youngest cohort disclosed their sexual identities at around age 16, whereas the oldest cohort reported disclosure around age 26 (Bishop et al., 2020). Similar trends are seen in gender-diverse populations, with younger generations disclosing their genders earlier and beginning social and medical transitions at younger ages (Puckett et al., 2021). These shifts, said Toomey, are likely due to the increased visibility of sexual and gender diversity in everyday life, as well as shifting attitudes that have become more positive toward SGD populations. Related to these earlier ages of identity development, the percentage of youth who identify as something other than cisgender or heterosexual is also larger than it was in prior generations (Conron, 2020). A 2020 poll found that while only 5 percent of the overall U.S. population identifies as lesbian, gay, bisexual, or transgender, this rises to 16 percent for those born between 1997 and 2002, and 10 percent for those born between 1981 and 1996 (Jones, 2021). These numbers, said Toomey, are consistent with other research showing that about 10 percent of youth aged 13–17 identify as LGBTQ (Conron, 2020). A survey of an incoming class at the University of Arizona, where Toomey teaches, found that 25 percent of students do not identify as heterosexual, and 12 percent identify outside the gender binary. In addition to the increasing numbers of LGBTQ youth,

---

[2] See http://www.generations-study.com.

the language they use to describe themselves is expanding and becoming more nuanced, said Toomey. For example, LGBTQ youth may identify themselves as plurisexual, bisexual, pansexual, queer, asexual, nonbinary, and/or transgender (Puckett et al., 2021; The Trevor Project, 2021b).

There is a considerable racial and ethnic diversity within the population of LGBTQ youth, said Allen Mallory (Ohio State University). Data from the Centers for Disease Control and Prevention Youth Risk Behavior Survey (CDC, 2021) show that, within each racial and ethnic group, 17–31 percent of youth identify as lesbian, gay, bisexual, or unsure about their sexual identities, or report sexual behavior with same-sex partners (Figure 1-1).

RESEARCH LANDSCAPE

Despite the growing and changing face of LGBTQ youth, research has not kept pace with the collective understanding of sexuality and gender, said Toomey. A 2014 study found that 86 percent of National Institutes of Health (NIH)-funded studies that examined LGBTQ health issues focused specifically on sexual-minority men, with only 13 percent focused on sexual-minority women and less than 7 percent on transgender populations (Coulter et al., 2014). Less than 10 percent of these studies focused on LGBTQ youth (Coulter et al., 2014). The health outcomes measured in NIH-funded studies were narrow, with 80 percent focused on HIV and AIDS, 30 percent on drug use, 23 percent on mental health, 16 percent on

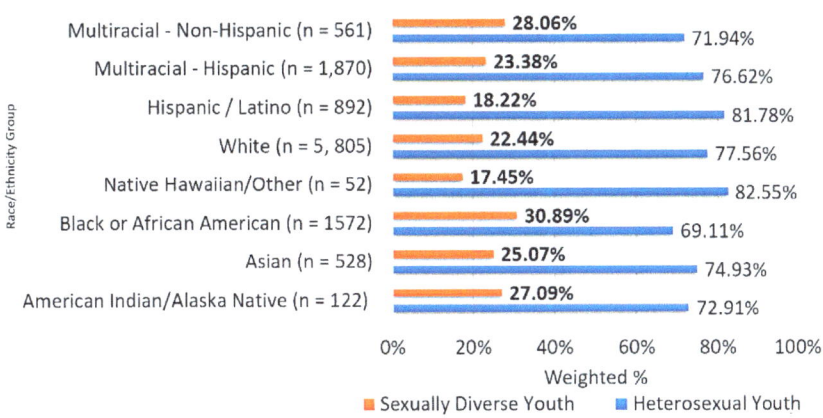

FIGURE 1-1 Racial diversity among sexually diverse youth (SDY).
SOURCE: Mallory presentation (2021).

sexual health, and 12.9 percent on alcohol use (Coulter et al., 2014). While many NIH-funded studies examined health disparities, said Toomey, less than 5 percent focused on malleable, systemic drivers of disparities or areas of leverage; such research is necessary to translate evidence into practice, policy, and intervention, he said.

In addition to these research gaps, even less is known about the unique experiences of diverse populations within the LGBTQ community, such as Black, Indigenous, people of color (BIPOC), plurisexual, and nonbinary individuals. These populations are underrepresented in research, despite evidence that large health disparities exist within these populations, said Toomey. Further, he said, research on sexual- and gender-diverse BIPOC populations tends to reify "racist notions of Black and Latinx youth as highly sexual beings and fails to acknowledge their holistic humanity." Research on well-being among asexual, intersex, and similar youth is "nearly nonexistent," said Toomey. The labels used within and among diverse LGBTQ populations are just beginning to be examined with empirical research, as are the intersections between sexuality and gender and characteristics such as race, ethnicity, immigration status, and disability.

The lack of inclusive questions about sexual and gender identity in large population-based surveys continues to create a barrier to understanding youth sexuality and gender development, as well as to identifying potential areas for intervention and prevention, said Toomey. Most of the research on these populations has been conducted by scientists who occupy privileged positions in society, said Toomey, including positions of educational privilege, socioeconomic privilege, and often racial and ethnic privilege. Historically, LGBTQ youth themselves have not been included in the production of knowledge in this area. Issues of representation and exclusion in research are not new, said Toomey, but they are systemic issues that will take systemic solutions to redirect, resolve, and repair. As a result of gaps and exclusions in research, said Toomey, the evidence base on LGBTQ youth is inconsistent and limited in areas. There is robust or growing evidence in areas such as gender-affirmative practices, school policies and practices, and some sexual health interventions (Abreu et al., 2021; Craig et al., 2019), but limited empirical literature in areas including mental health interventions, family-based interventions, and multilevel interventions (Bochicchio et al., 2020; Coulter et al., 2019; Newcomb et al., 2019; Hobaica et al., 2018).

The evidence base on LGBTQ youth is also limited due to a lack of research that incorporates an intersectional perspective, said Mallory. Every individual has multiple overlapping and interacting identities; these identities include characteristics such as race, ethnicity, gender, sexual orientation, religion, and abilities. These characteristics are tied to social systems that structure society and empower certain identities as privileged and others as disadvantaged, and that also impact a person's day-to-day experiences of advantage, privilege, and power. When research focuses on individual identities (e.g., sexual orientation), the emphasis is put on attributes of groups of people, rather than on the systemic inequality, stigma, and discrimination that can lead to disparities in health and well-being, said Mallory. An intersectional perspective, on the other hand, goes beyond categories of identity to examine how macro- and micro-systems shape individual and community experiences. There are myriad ways in which these systems may interact, said Mallory, and there are three hypotheses currently being explored: the multiplicative, additive, and inuring hypotheses (Mallory and Russell, 2021; Else-Quest and Hyde, 2016a, 2016b; Thoma and Huebner, 2013; Raver and Nishii, 2010). Mallory used the relationship between discrimination and mental health to demonstrate each hypothesis (Figure 1-2). The multiplicative hypothesis proposes that, for each additional form of discrimination a person experiences, mental health would multiplicatively worsen (i.e., two forms of discrimination worsen mental health twice as much as one form of discrimination). The additive hypothesis suggests that mental health incrementally worsens for each additional form of discrimination experienced. The inuring hypothesis suggests that, after experiencing one form of discrimination, additional forms of discrimination do not worsen mental health. Mallory noted that while his examples focused on

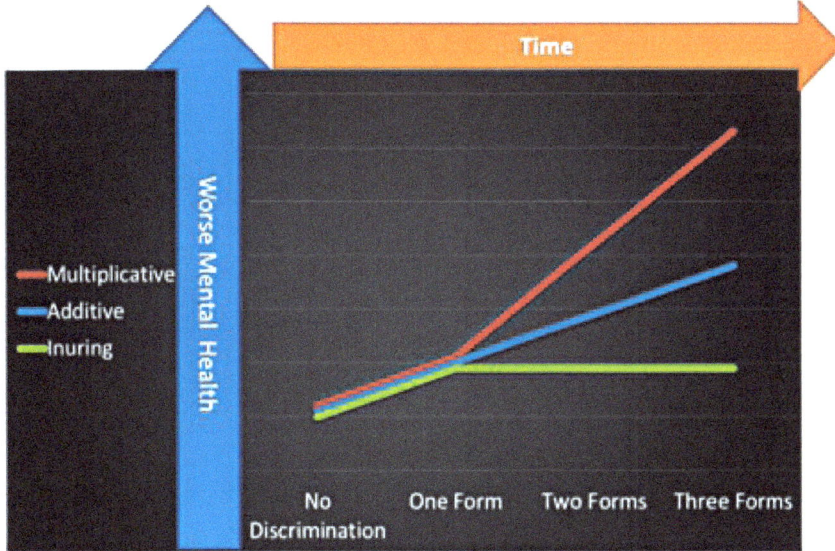

FIGURE 1-2 Intersectional hypotheses.
SOURCE: Mallory presentation (2021).

discrimination, the same hypotheses could be applicable for examining protective factors (e.g., engagement with multiple communities) in the lives of SGD youth.

There is ongoing debate among scholars and researchers about how to best integrate or represent intersectionality in research with SGD youth, said Mallory. One critical characteristic, however, is that intersectional research explicitly addresses intersectional power, inequality, privilege, and/or disadvantage. Research that does not address intersectional power, inequality, privilege and/or disadvantage does not fully align with intersectionality theory, and research that does not align with intersectionality theory, he said, has clear limitations for understanding the experiences of SGD youth. Researchers could improve their work by asking themselves who they have missed or failed to include, and who has been actively excluded from their research. Further, Mallory said that researchers should consider whether they are asking the questions that matter to SGD youth, and whether the questions truly reflect the intersections of their experiences and identities. Mallory emphasized the importance of research that can identify positive intersectional experiences, as well as negative ones. For example, two recent daily diary studies found that participants (Black and Muslim SGD youth) reported more positive than negative experiences (e.g., seeing their particular intersectional identities represented in the media) (Jackson et al., 2021). These types of positive intersectional experiences are largely nonexistent in the current literature, he said. While research is acknowledging and finding ways to incorporate the intersecting identities and experiences of SGD youth into research, there is more work to be done.

POLICY LANDSCAPE

In reviewing the policy landscape facing LGBTQ youth, Naomi Goldberg (Movement Advancement Project) emphasized the importance of recognizing the incredible gender diversity, sexual diversity, and racial and ethnic diversity in this population. It is critical to consider which youths may be disproportionately impacted by anti-LGBTQ policies and which are particularly privileged by LGBTQ-affirming policies, she said. Goldberg also highlighted the fact that youths are engaged in multiple systems, including schools, faith communities, the child welfare system, and the healthcare system, and the policies that govern these systems shape the experiences of the young people involved. Policy is a broad term, encompassing federal laws; state laws; local, city, county, and district ordinances and policies; agency regulations; and funding decisions.

Goldberg summarized the key laws and policies that impact LGBTQ youth, starting with laws and policies that explicitly and directly implicate sexual orientation and gender identity. In the school environment, these policies may cover issues including nondiscrimination, bullying, curriculum, and participation and access (e.g., to sports or certain facilities). In the healthcare arena, policies that directly impact LGBTQ youth include insurance coverage determinations, nondiscrimination, whether providers may refuse service, and permitting or prohibiting certain procedures or approaches (e.g., conversion therapy, gender-affirming care). Government policies may include anti-discrimination rules, the availability of religious exemptions, and more. There are many laws and policies that directly impact LGBTQ youth, and there has been considerable movement in this area in recent years, said Goldberg. For example, many states have passed laws banning the use of conversion therapy.[3] Currently, half of the states in the U.S. either ban conversion therapy outright or have restrictions in place on its use, and many cities and counties have also banned this therapy. At the same time, she said, hundreds of bills have been introduced in state legislatures to place restrictions on transgender youth, including bans on participation in sports, limited access to bathrooms that match gender identity, and reduced access to affirming medical care. In the past year, eight states have passed laws restricting trans youth's ability to play sports, and Arkansas banned affirming medical care. Looking across many areas of LGBTQ youth-related laws and policies, Goldberg also noted trends in state policies across the country, which vary significantly by region (Figure 1-3). States in the South and Midwest tend to have more anti-LGBTQ policies than affirming or supportive policies, while states in the West, Northeast, and upper Midwest have more affirming policies than anti-LGBTQ policies, said Goldberg.

Goldberg emphasized the importance of remembering that policies impact individual people, and that they may not impact all LGBTQ youth in the same way. Both the academic literature and the experiences of young people, she said, show that there is a direct connection between the policy landscape and the experiences of LGBTQ youth. For example, in places with enumerated school nondiscrimination and anti-bullying policies, students report feeling safer, hearing fewer homophobic remarks, experiencing less victimization based on their sexual orientation or gender identity, and having higher self-esteem. They are also less likely to be absent from school (Meyer et al., 2019; Kosciw et al., 2018; Berger et al., 2017; Hall, 2017; Greytak et al., 2016; Kull et al., 2016; Hatzenbuehler et al., 2014; Hatzenbuehler and Keyes, 2013; Kosciw et al., 2013; Wheeler Black et al., 2012; Hatzenbuehler, 2011; Russell et al., 2010; Horn and Szalacha, 2009; Goodenow et al., 2006). Schools with supportive environments—including inclusive curricula, suicide-prevention programming, and affirming staff—

---

[3] Conversion therapy is any attempt to change a person's sexual orientation, gender identity, or gender expression (GLAAD, n.d.).

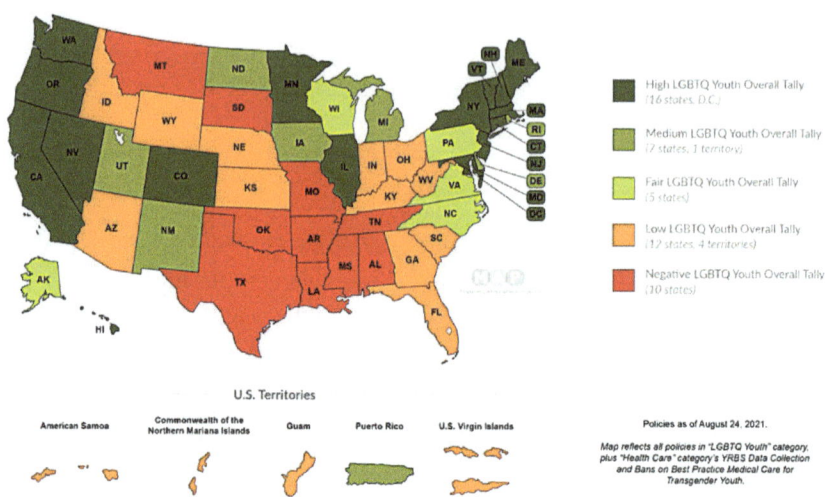

FIGURE 1-3 Patchwork of youth policies.
SOURCE: Goldberg presentation (2021).

also improve students' mental health (The Trevor Project, 2021a). On the other hand, policies that negatively target LGBTQ youth have a negative impact on their mental health and well-being (GLSEN, 2018), said Goldberg. Even when anti-LGBTQ proposals do not become law, the discussion of LGBTQ lives in the public sphere can have negative effects; for example, on calls with staff from The Trevor Project and Trans Lifeline, Goldberg heard reports of spikes in calls to crisis lines when media stories negatively focus on trans youth playing sports (see also Levesque, 2021).

In addition to laws that explicitly implicate LGBTQ youth, there are many more policies that are critical to the health, safety, and development of these young people, said Goldberg. For example, LGBTQ youth, particularly youth of color, are overrepresented in the child welfare system and the juvenile justice system. Thus, laws and policies about policing, law enforcement, child welfare, community safety, families, and education are critically important to LGBTQ youth. Moving forward, said Goldberg, it is vitally important to meaningfully include youth voices at the table and to empower LGBTQ youth to be a part of crafting the policies that impact their lives. She noted that this could include establishing youth advisory councils, identifying youth advisors, engaging in problem-solving exercises with young people, and using funding strategies that involve young people in the development of policies and programs.

REFLECTIONS

Following the speaker presentations, Russell led participants in a discussion to reflect on the presentations and the broader workshop aims. He asked participants to identify one takeaway they hoped would emerge from the workshop. These ideas included:

- Ensuring the inclusion of LGBTQ people in policymaking at the highest levels (Goldberg);
- Finding ways to be inclusive of the diversity of SGD youth experiences and identities (Mallory);
- Considering the ways that nonLGBTQ-specific policies shape the intersectional experiences of LGBTQ youth (Toomey);
- Reducing and minimizing the power structures that are present in research science, and actively including young people in the knowledge-production process from day one (Toomey);
- Recognizing that many of the laws and policies that impact LGBTQ youth are built on the same white supremacist framework as other laws and policies, and reconsidering how to define concepts such as safety, security, and well-being (Goldberg).

A workshop participant asked the speakers to comment on funding priorities for LGBTQ health equity, research, and practice. Goldberg responded that there are many innovative and groundbreaking programs happening around the country; for example, a program in Michigan brings together LGBTQ youth advocates, state officials, and child welfare professionals to help families understand gender diversity in small children. Funding is needed, she said, to share, adapt, and scale up these programs for use in other parts of the country. Mallory concurred and stressed the importance of developing models to help SGD youth, such as the Stories and Numbers project.[4] There are well-funded efforts that push for anti-LGBTQ school policies, said Toomey, and there is a need for funding and for a national strategy to counter these efforts and to advocate for evidence-based policies and practices in schools.

---

[4] See https://storiesandnumbers.org.

2

LGBTQ Youth of Color

In the key concepts and framing session, Allen Mallory emphasized the significant racial and ethnic diversity among LGBTQ youth. Russell Toomey noted that, despite progress in some areas, disparities between LGBTQ youth of color and cisgender, heterosexual youth continue to increase. LGBTQ youth are overrepresented in the child welfare and juvenile justice systems, and this overrepresentation is particularly acute for LGBTQ youth of color, said Naomi Goldberg. Despite this overrepresentation the experiences and perspectives of LGBTQ youth of color are often absent from research and policy development, said Mallory; in particular, the effects of the intersectional nature of systems, stigma, and discrimination on this population are poorly understood.

This chapter brings together insights from two panels aimed at highlighting these issues by focusing on outcomes and interventions for LGBTQ youth of color. In the first panel, LGBTQ youth of color discussed barriers and solutions to support well-being; this panel was followed by presentations on the state of research on, and services to support, the well-being of LGBTQ youth of color.

LIVED EXPERTISE

Planning committee member Nat Duran (Illinois Safe Schools Alliance) served as moderator of the Lived Expertise panel and guided the discussion through a series of questions as listed below. The panelists were Manal Vishnoi (Northbrook Pride Youth Program), A.J. Valdez (El Paso, Texas), Malcolm Lin (University of Kansas), and Zara Khan (Chicago, Illinois).

How Do You Define Health and Well-Being?

Vishnoi said that they consider health and well-being to be a combination of many components, including mental health, physical health, community health, and social support systems. Valdez defined health and well-being as being composed of one's physical and mental state. Lin said that it is "the ability to live and be a prosperous, happy person." Finally, Khan defined health as a person's mental, physical, and emotional state of being, and said that well-being is when "someone is in a comfortable state of being."

What Are Promising Solutions to Inequalities in Health and Well-Being That You Have Seen Work in Your Communities?

In August 2019, replied Valdez, there was a mass shooting in El Paso, Texas. Out of this tragedy came the El Paso United Family Resiliency Center, which offers free counseling to people of all ages, backgrounds, and creeds. Valdez emphasized the value of this center, suggesting similar centers should be opened in communities across the country. Vishnoi agreed with this idea and added that physical health services could also be offered at these centers, because many people cannot afford healthcare otherwise. Lin emphasized the need for access to healthcare, arguing that people should not need to drive for over 20 minutes to see a doctor. Lin said that each community may need more than one center so that people can be seen without long emergency room wait times. In addition to ensuring access, said Khan, it is critical to educate communities about mental, emotional, and physical health. Khan said that, as an Asian-American, she has observed harmful stigma in her community around mental health; educating people and providing healthcare resources would be very helpful. Specifically, she said, discussing "self-care" as a concept of everyday wellness, rather than as a luxury or self-indulgence, could help people see self-care as achievable for everyone. Valdez agreed, saying that self-care can be as simple as relaxing at home. Vishnoi proposed that topics such as self-care and mental health should be included in the curricula of health classes.

What Are the Barriers to These Types of Solutions?

One of the biggest barriers to the suggested solutions, said Lin, is that many people do not know how to help a person who is different from a "standard White person." Lin said that some mental health professionals are unsure of how to approach a person with an unfamiliar issue, or someone who is a "kind of person" they haven't encountered before; for example, there is an expectation that everyone has a loving, caring family and enough food to eat.

These barriers make it more difficult for people of color or people who are different to get help. Vishnoi added that many health systems are built to work against people of color and LGBTQ people of color, specifically. For example, internalized bias from providers can negatively impact the experiences of LGBTQ people of color within the health system. Kahn agreed, noting that some health issues, such as mental health, are not always visible. For people who are already marginalized, she said, "society doesn't always listen." Kahn emphasized the importance of believing people when they express how they are feeling. Vishnoi noted that, while many health organizations have attempted to address these issues by establishing a diversity board or hiring a diverse person, health systems require systemic change to better serve LGBTQ people of color.

Who Are the Influential People in Your Community and How Can We Support Them?

Parents and families have a considerable influence on young people, said Khan, and rejection of LGBTQ youth by their families can lead to negative consequences, including isolation and higher suicide rates. Khan suggested that healthcare providers or schools could provide resources and education to parents to help them better understand, support, and validate their LGBTQ children. When parents are not supportive, said Valdez, young people can receive support and validation in a supportive school environment. The first foundational step to changing the school culture, he said, is putting anti-discrimination policies in place to mitigate future discrimination and opposition to identity-affirming programs. Vishnoi said that schoolteachers and counselors can have a large influence on both students' experiences in school as well as on their lives post-graduation. Allies in education could receive training to better prepare them to function as trusted adults for all types of students, Vishnoi suggested. Valdez added that teachers who take part in LGBTQ advocacy in schools need support from the administration and other higher-ups, particularly in communities where these activities can be controversial. Lin concurred that teachers and counselors are extremely important, and said that one of the best ways to support them would be to increase educators' pay. Teachers are "the reason that we are who we are today."

If You Had a Magic Wand, What System Would You Change and How?

Lin said that they would change the mental health system to give mental health professionals a broader mindset about how they can help people and how to simplify the process for patients. Valdez and Khan offered ideas for changes in the educational system. Valdez would redesign schools so that teachers recognize and work with the various ways that students learn, while Khan would want students to learn about their rights, both inside and outside of school, and would make sex education curricula more inclusive (e.g., normalize asexuality). Vishnoi went a step further, saying that "all of those systems need to be torn down and built back up." The systems were built to serve White, cisgender people, Vishnoi said, and they need to be rebuilt with young people, people of color, LGBTQ people, and other marginalized people in mind to effectively serve and support these communities.

What Are Common Misconceptions About Youth?

Many adults, said Vishnoi, have internalized the idea that youth are "stupid." Vishnoi said that if adults took the time to listen to young people, they would realize that youth are smart, can understand complex ideas, and often know what they need. This attitude, Vishnoi said, prevents systems from serving youth properly. Valdez agreed, saying that adults often see youth as naïve or ignorant. He said that all people, regardless of age, should treat one another with respect and aim to respectfully discuss differences. Valdez stressed that respect should go both ways, and that while adults are sometimes not as respectful or attentive as they should be, teenagers can also lack respect and attentiveness. Another misconception, said Khan, is that youth are not capable or responsible. Khan drew attention to the magnitude of student and youth activism and noted that many political and social movements are predominantly youth led. Kahn suggested that youth need opportunities to learn the skills of advocacy and social change. Lin said that adults commonly think that their time and their responsibilities are more important than those of youths. Lin remarked that disregard for the value of youth time and youth priorities is a key reason why many young people do not want to work or return to school. Vishnoi agreed with Lin and said that "a lot of adults see youth of color as lazy, uncaring, and not having any ambition," and that this is partly due to adults dismissing the priorities of youth. This view of youth of color, Lin said, is a harmful misconception and can be difficult for young people to overcome. Further, said Lin, this view can contribute to pay inequality and discrimination in hiring, which furthers existing disparities.

How Does Your Racial or Ethnic Identity Shape the Way You Experience Your Sexual Orientation and/or Gender Identity?

"I grew up in a very, very White town," said Vishnoi. As a person who is half Indian and half White, a feeling of isolation resulted from not knowing many people with a South Asian identity. "Being alone in that way," Vishnoi said, helped them to more quickly realize that they were nonbinary and what that meant. Because Vishnoi already felt excluded from many things, feeling excluded from womanhood was not a new or unique feeling.

Valdez was a "stereotypical football player," so coming out was a "big shock to everyone." While coming out to his Mexican-American family was "rocky" at first, his family is now "completely supportive." After coming out, Valdez's father told him, "Since the day you were born, I was your first and last line of protection against anything, and now I'm even more so your first and last line of protection against anything or anyone."

"I grew up very stereotypically Asian," said Lin. When Lin came out, their parents did not believe they were nonbinary or pansexual. "They shoved everything about me as a person under a rug," said Lin, which felt "very disheartening and painful." Taiwan, where Lin's family is from, was one of the first countries to support LGBTQ rights. This led Lin to believe that they would be safe coming out to their parents, but their parents responded in a very "old fashioned" way. Because of this, Lin is very self-protective and tries to "stay away from things [if] I know I'm going to get hurt."

Khan's parents are both from India, but they were not very socially conservative. When Khan came out, there were people who told them that it was "not possible to be Indian and also to be a member of the LGBTQ community." Historically, Indian culture was open to LGBTQ people, said Khan, until Victorian era reforms in the 1860s began repressing "anyone who was not cis or straight." Coming out as an LGBTQ individual who is Indian American has resulted in a "lot of push and pull between different identities," Khan said.

How Do You Think COVID-19 Has Impacted LGBTQ Young People and the Community as a Whole?

Duran noted that there were concerns that the isolation during the COVID-19 pandemic would lead to negative consequences for LGBTQ youth. However, anecdotes suggest that some young people are feeling more empowered: Valdez's GSA club[1] has seen enormous growth, and his school district has received an unprecedented number of gender-support plan requests. Duran asked for panelists' thoughts on the impact of COVID-19 on LGBTQ youth. Vishnoi said that the pandemic provided a lot of time to self-reflect and gave young people "the space to really explore their identities." Valdez agreed, noting that the beginning of the pandemic had an emotional impact that led to him coming out. Khan added that the pandemic also encouraged people to connect in virtual communities, and

---

[1] The clubs were formerly known as Gay-Straight Alliances; now they are referred to either as Genders & Sexualities Alliances or simply GSAs.

that some people were able to interact, for the first time, with people who have similar identities. Valdez reported that, although his high school is fairly conservative, a large number of students have come out recently—he estimates that "maybe a fifth or fourth of the entire school is now out." This shift is visible, with students adopting "a completely different style and ... aesthetics." While the isolation of COVID-19 was difficult, "we came back stronger," Valdez said. The GSA at his school is part of a "little political revolution," and aims not just to help LGBTQ-identified students, but to bring the entire student body together. In closing, Valdez urged young people to "use [your voice] and run with fire."

RESEARCH LANDSCAPE

There are a number of patterns of inequality evident in the literature on LGBTQ youth of color, said Carlos Santos (University of California Los Angeles). LGBTQ youth of color are at greater risk of HIV infection (Balaji et al., 2013; Celentano et al., 2006), they are more likely to lack access to information about HIV/AIDS (Voisin et al., 2013; Mustanski et al., 2011), and they are less likely to know their HIV status or follow up with appropriate medical care compared to White, non-Latino, sexual-minority youth (Magnus et al., 2010). The mental health literature is mixed, said Santos, with some studies suggesting that LGBTQ youth of color experience greater mental health problems compared to Whites, others finding that they experience fewer mental health problems, and still others finding no difference (Toomey et al., 2017). Mono-racial samples have found evidence of poorer mental health among LGBTQ youth of color (Fields et al., 2015). There is also evidence of differences between LGBTQ youth of color and White youth in terms of substance use; for example, one study found more negative sexual health consequences of drinking among Black LGBTQ youth (Burns et al., 2015).

With this background, Santos turned to the limitations of the literature on the well-being of LGBTQ youth of color. He emphasized the importance of adopting an intersectionality framework for research on this population, and he outlined some of the critical aspects of such a framework. First, he said, researchers should avoid focusing on social identities alone. While identities are important, they are only one part of a complex story. It is essential to capture the oppressions that are associated with social identities (e.g., racism, heterosexism), and how these oppressive forces overlap to create unique conditions. As an illustration, Santos asked workshop participants to imagine reading Sojourner Truth's "Ain't I a Woman" without the context of the oppressive forces of racism or sexism. Further, he said, effective research will consider how oppressive forces and social identities are experienced both contextually and relationally, and how measurement and design might best capture the contextual and relational nature of the experiences of LGBTQ youth of color. Santos emphasized that not all oppressions are the same. Anti-blackness and anti-indigeneity are foundational social, political, and economic forces in the history of the U.S., he said, and they need to be centered in studies of LGBTQ youth of color. Anti-blackness, racism, and colorism should be central to any study that purports to adopt an intersectionality framework, said Santos. Further, the role of state-sponsored status and legality are also critical to examine when studying the experiences of those with ties to other nation states.

One barrier to studying and capturing intersectional phenomena is a lack of intersectional measures in the field. One approach, he said, may be to adapt existing measures; for example, Lewis and colleagues (2017) adapted an existing racial identity scale to measure gender racial identity. Similarly, Sarno and colleagues (2021) have developed measures to capture perceived racism in the lesbian, gay, and bisexual (LGB) community and feelings of conflict in sexual- and gender-minority people of color's allegiance to their ethnic-racial and sexual-minority identities. Using adapted measures, VanDaalen and Santos (2017) found that Asian-American participants perceived higher levels of racism in the LGB community than did Latinx participants. Santos encouraged researchers to consider intersectional issues across multiple systems and levels of systems. For example, LGBTQ youth experiences may be shaped by microsystems such as perceived racism or conflicts between multiple social identities, mesosystems such as lack of access to culturally sensitive health providers, and macrosystems such as state laws and policies. Santos also encouraged researchers to adopt frameworks that connect intersecting dimensions of resilience; for example, considering questions such as, "How does Black liberation tie to the neurodiversity movement for LGBTQ black youth who may live with disabilities?"

Finally, Santos encouraged researchers to work with LGBTQ communities using methods like the community-based participatory research framework. Santos suggested that issues can arise when research is performed in these communities without involvement of individuals from these communities in the planning, design, or implementation of a study. While representation does not solve all problems associated with researching historically minoritized and marginalized communities, he said, representation still matters. Beyond involving community members in research, researchers should consider how to channel resources toward community groups that are doing critical work, rather than funding people who are already in privileged positions.

EXPLORING RACISM AND SEXUAL IDENTITY DURING THE COVID-19 PANDEMIC

Karina Gattamorta (University of Miami) presented information on the impact of racism and family rejection on sexual- and gender-minority (SGM) stressors and mental health. At the start of the COVID-19 pandemic, said Gattamorta, SGM students were hypothesized to be a hyper-vulnerable population, due in part to the potential of returning to homes where they could face elevated stressors, such as family rejection and identity concealment. An online survey examined the relationship between these types of stressors and mental health among SGM college students during the COVID-19 pandemic. Gattamorta described how the data from the survey were used to examine two issues: first, changes in frequency of racism and SGM-related stress since the start of the pandemic and whether these factors led to psychological distress; second, relationships between racism, family rejection, identity concealment, and internalized homophobia. Gattamorta noted that the study was guided by both the intersectionality framework and the minority stress framework. The researchers utilized a number of existing tools to measure racism, SGM stressors, and psychological distress, and they adapted these tools to specifically examine changes during the pandemic.

The first study, said Gattamorta, aimed to answer three questions:

1. Whether, since the start of the COVID-19 pandemic, increased frequency of racism and SGM stressors predicts current psychological distress;
2. How, since the start of the pandemic, the relationship between increased SGM stressors and current psychological distress changes when adjusting for experiences of racism; and
3. Whether, since the start of the pandemic, increased racism moderates the associations between increased SGM stressors and current psychological distress.

Young adulthood is a time of vulnerability for poor mental health, particularly for SGMs (Fish, 2020; Fish et al., 2019, 2020), and COVID-19 has had a disproportionate impact on communities of color (Czeisler et al., 2020; Liu and Modir, 2020; Moore et al., 2020). It was hypothesized, said Gattamorta, that students who hold both racial and SGM identities may have compounding experiences of vulnerability due to the COVID-19 pandemic. The data showed that the independent effects of increases in racism, family rejection, internalized homophobia, internalized transphobia, and identity concealment were all associated with greater psychological distress. When controlling for racism, the associations held but were somewhat attenuated. However, the moderating effects of increased racism on the associations between each SGM stressor and psychological distress were not statistically significant.

The second study focused specifically on the two stressors of family rejection and racism. Of the approximately 200 students in the sample, 65 percent reported increased family rejection during the pandemic, and 67.5 percent experienced an increased in racism. The study sought to examine the impact of changes in the external stressors of family rejection and racism on the internal stressors of internalized homophobia and identity concealment. The data showed that all four of the measured stressors were significantly and positively related to each other, said Gattamorta. For example, experiencing both increased family rejection and increased racism was significantly associated with a greater likelihood of experiencing increased identity concealment compared to experiencing either racism or family rejection alone, or no stressors at all.

These studies and others make clear, said Gattamorta, that racism and SGM-related stressors have a unique impact on mental health. It is critical, she said, that universities and mental health stakeholders acknowledge and address these stressors, particularly in the context of the COVID-19 pandemic. Gattamorta offered three suggestions for how this could be realized: (1) increase access to affirming and culturally sensitive mental health services and providers, both on and off campus; (2) increase training and resources to ensure a public and mental health workforce that is well equipped to address needs related to racism and SGM stressors; and (3) increase engagement of SGM students of color in mental health services through affirming practices and allyship.

SYSTEMS OF SUPPORT

The individuals who are "pushed to the side" at other youth-focused organizations are the ones that the Ruth Ellis Center and Trans Sistas of Color Project focus on reaching, said Lilianna Reyes (Ruth Ellis Center). Specifically, these organizations reach out to Black and Brown youths who are homeless, may not be in school, and who often do not have access to other agencies or resources. The Ruth Ellis Center is Michigan's largest lesbian, gay, bisexual, and transgender (LGBT) homeless youth services organization; it offers services including a drop-in center, hot meals, and a closet. In addition, this organization works with the Trans Sistas of Color Project to help trans individuals get their names and gender markers changed. The center is currently building the first ever LGBT long-term supportive housing shelter in Detroit, which will allow young people to stay as long as they need, said Reyes.

When the COVID-19 pandemic began, the Ruth Ellis Center had to adapt its procedures. While many organizations shifted their services online, this approach was not feasible for the Center's clients, many of whom did not have homes or access to electricity or Wi-Fi. The Center held meetings outdoors, started delivering food, and offered technology to those who needed it. Reyes noted that many Black and Brown community members gathered regardless of the COVID-19 restrictions, because "the thought of being isolated and not being around the people and family that you love was scarier than getting COVID." The center did its best to practice harm reduction and to "meet folks where they were at."

The Ruth Ellis Center is based on the idea that young people should have a voice in every aspect of the organization, and that a youth can and should one day become the executive director or board president. "We don't just say that and throw it to the wind, we really believe it," said Reyes. All of Reyes' current staff are from the community, and started out as youths who were homeless, receiving services at the center, or part of the associated healthcare center. These youths may have difficulty getting other jobs because of criminal background checks, inaccurate names or gender markers, or a lack of a high school or college diploma. The Ruth Ellis Center helps people gain the skills and resources they need to be successful, and holds the belief that the best people to serve the community are people from the community itself. The Ruth Ellis Center takes a housing-first approach, but views housing as not just a physical space but also a frame of mind: "where you feel safe and where home is." The center focuses on undoing racism and considers the intersection of identities in the community. Reyes said that "when you center the most marginalized, everyone benefits."

Reyes noted that trans women of color are one of the most marginalized and vulnerable communities, and the Trans Sistas of Color Project was established to uplift this community. Trans Sistas of Color helps the community by providing emergency assistance for individuals, conducting policy work to facilitate gender changes, and supporting families when a trans woman is murdered. Many young trans women with unstable housing turn to sex work, said Reyes, noting the potential dangers. The Ruth Ellis Center and the Trans Sistas of Color Project work with these girls and women to "help them figure out what lifestyle they want to lead" and to support them along the way.

REFLECTIONS

Following the presentations, planning committee member Amorie Robinson (Ruth Ellis Center) led a question-and-answer session with the panelists. Workshop audience members were invited to submit questions for panelists via the virtual livestream. Robinson began with an observation that individuals who are gender nonconforming can sometimes get "lost in the data"—their experiences can be overlooked in research and practice. These youths—such as those who are perceived to be gay, feminine-presenting boys and masculine-presenting girls—are likely to be targets of anti-LGBTQ attacks and are prone to mental health risk factors, she said. Robinson asked speakers to comment on ways to provide support, understanding, and protection for these youths. Gattamorta agreed with Robinson's assessment, noting that researchers tend to "lump" together racial and ethnic minority or SGM populations, despite unique experiences. One issue, she said, is that small sample sizes lead to a lack of statistical power when trying to examine these groups. It can be difficult to access a sufficient number of participants from marginalized populations, Gattamorta said, and there is a need for more research in this area. Santos added that intersectionality-inspired research needs to focus on addressing the needs of those who are the most likely to experience the deleterious effects of being historically minoritized and marginalized. When these voices are centered, it can change the types of research questions, approaches, and measures that are used.

A workshop participant asked speakers to address the issue of balancing efforts to build resiliency among LGBTQ youth of color with efforts to hold institutions accountable for their roles in harming or failing to support LGBTQ youth of color. Reyes responded with the suggestion that these activities be pursued in tandem. She said that the Ruth Ellis Center originally focused only on individuals, and on building up resiliency so that young people could better navigate the obstacles and oppressions they faced. As the Center gained more capacity and experience, it began working on pushing back against systems themselves. Challenging racism and other oppressions on a systemic level, said Reyes, requires being comfortable with conflict and with the discomfort of others, and using one's privilege to push for change. In addition, she noted, having the support of the board and other decision makers is critical for navigating difficult conversations and holding people accountable. For example, if a funder takes actions that are "not conducive to the liberation of Black and Brown people," the organization may have to reject that source of funding, said Reyes.

Another workshop participant asked for ideas for how services and researchers that focus on youth of color can be more inclusive of LGBTQ youth, and how those that focus on LGBTQ populations can be more inclusive of youth of color. Gattamorta responded that it is essential for research and intervention design to be informed by the community, and for community members to be empowered to participate at all stages. She recalled that the panel of LGBTQ youth spoke about the importance of listening to young people and giving them space to have a voice in work that affects their own lives. Santos added that there are several benefits to using a community-based participatory research framework, and that it is important to go beyond paying lip services to participatory research and to meaningfully engage with the community at every step of the research process.

Robinson next asked the panelists how to reach and engage with LGBTQ youth and their family members who do not understand or accept an LGBTQ child. This group, she said, likely includes many young Black and Brown people who need protection in their homes, schools, and communities. Reyes replied that "family of origin is sometimes where the biggest trauma happens," and that it is not always possible or appropriate to have family unification as a goal. She emphasized the importance of not only considering ways to support and engage biological families, but also of looking at the role that chosen family can play. She explained that when we broaden our definition of family, we have more resources to draw upon in supporting LGBTQ youth. Santos added that one approach for engaging with people is to highlight how intersecting forms of oppression and privilege impact every individual. For example, as a queer Latino individual, Santos is subject to the forces of heterosexism and racism, but he also experiences privileges as a cisgender man. Having conversations about the intersections between various identities and related oppressive forces can help people better understand and be more mindful of their positions in society, and thus provide a framework for exploration of these issues.

The topic of outcomes and well-being for LGBTQ youth of color was also raised in another workshop session focused on existing research on inequalities, prevention, and intervention. In the question-and-answer session, planning committee member David Chae (Tulane University) asked speakers to comment on the role of racism within LGBTQ contexts, specifically sexual racism in gay communities and gay online spaces, as a potential cause of racial inequities in health and HIV. John Pachankis (Yale School of Public Health) responded that large nationwide surveys showed that perceived discrimination within the gay community is a more robust predictor of the mental health of young gay and bisexual men than traditional minority stressors such as stigma, bullying, and family rejection. Chae said that one concept that can be used to explain this is "invisibilization," in which a person is invisible within his or her own community; Chae said this experience is largely driven by racism. José Bauermeister (University of Pennsylvania) added that racism in these spaces has an impact on physical health as well; the racialized sexualization in online spaces shapes the sexual network of these communities and impacts how HIV is spread. Bianca Wilson (University of California) noted that racism also has a major impact on how the LGBTQ community thinks about young people in state systems such as foster care. There is a tendency, said Wilson, for people to see the overrepresentation of LGBTQ youth in state systems and think, "We need to get those terrible parents of color to stop rejecting their youth." However, the data show that most LGBTQ youth of color enter state systems prior to identifying as LGBTQ. Increased state surveillance of Black and Brown communities filters children into the foster care system, explained Wilson. There is a racist element, she said, in the close scrutiny of Black and Brown families and there is a lack of attention to the structural racism that underlies the foster care system.

As a follow-up, Chae asked speakers to imagine what an intervention for reducing racial inequalities within LGBTQ youth contexts might look like. Bauermeister responded that he was not sure about a specific intervention, but that there is a need for greater investment in multilevel strategies. While there are various places where interventions can and do happen, he said, they tend to happen in siloes. Instead, we need multidisciplinary projects that coordinate and build distinct types of interventions in different kinds of spaces and that focus not just on young people but also on the people in their social ecology. Bauermeister acknowledged that this was a "big ask" and would require significant financial resources; he suggested that federal agencies such as the National Institutes of Health and the Centers for Disease Control and Prevention might contribute toward this type of initiative. He also stressed that the interventions themselves are most effective when they are flexible and adapted to the needs of unique communities. Wilson concurred and said that multilevel approaches can target structural determinants of health, rather than simply acknowledging their existence. As an example, Wilson described an intervention her colleagues developed to improve the health of HIV-positive Black gay and bisexual men, which provides legal assistance to challenge housing discrimination and discrimination in other contexts. Much of the intervention is still focused on the individual level, she said, but it also seeks to change individuals' relationships to the structural-level issues that we tend to name but not directly target for change.

3

Promising Interventions in Personal, Carceral, and Care Systems

On the second day of the workshop, speakers, and participants discussed the current status of LGBTQ youth in state systems, including foster care and juvenile justice; examined research in this area and potential areas for action; and identified promising interventions.

LANDSCAPE: OUTCOMES, INEQUALITIES, AND KNOWN INTERVENTIONS

LGBTQ young people are disproportionately represented in multiple state-based systems, said Sarah Mountz (University at Albany). LGBTQ youth make up 19–34 percent of young people in foster care systems and 12–20 percent of youths in the juvenile justice system; the majority of these youths are young people of color. In both systems, high rates of sexual victimization and harassment are reported both inside and outside the facilities, said Mountz. Within the foster care system, LGBTQ youth are twice as likely to be placed in congregate-care facilities like group homes, they experience more movement while in care, and they are more likely to report being treated poorly within the system. LGBTQ youth in foster care face mental health and substance abuse disparities, educational disparities, and heightened barriers when they age out of the system. Within the juvenile justice system, said Bianca Wilson (UCLA), LGBTQ youth are kept in custody longer and experience more sexual victimization by their peers. Over half of girls in juvenile justice facilities identify as sexual minorities, said Wilson. The foster care and juvenile justice systems are interconnected, said Wilson, with youths in detention more likely to have a history of foster care (Irvine and Canfield, 2016).

Paired with the knowledge that schools are often hostile spaces for LGBTQ youth and youth of color (see Chapter 6), Mountz called the movement between systems a "revolving door." Young people are shuttled between settings that fail to nurture and support them, and that criminalize their survival skills and community-building efforts. The impacts for child welfare and juvenile justice system-involved youths, said Mountz, are poorer health and wellness outcomes, lack of access to opportunities, ensnarement in punitive systems, exposure to interpersonal and state violence, and impaired transitions to adulthood. Despite these disparities and challenges, Mountz noted that these youths can flourish and become leaders in community initiatives that provide support and networks for themselves and others.

Wilson identified several existing interventions that can reduce disparities for child welfare and juvenile justice system-involved LGBTQ youth. However, she noted the lack of a strong empirical base for the programs and interventions being implemented. Some sites are both implementing and evaluating initiatives (e.g., Alameda County, Allegheny County), but there is a need for more research on interventions in this area. Wilson looked at interventions on three levels. First, interventions can target individuals who have direct interactions with young people, such as social workers, case managers, and officers in detention facilities. Second, interventions can try to make organizational and structural changes in the systems themselves. At the individual level, Wilson noted that there is often an overreliance on one-time trainings and an absence of ongoing coaching and structural support. Addressing these lacks could improve the capacities of individuals. At the organizational level, she noted the importance focusing on synergies between existing initiatives and new interventions. In addition, she said, a more thorough understanding of the current reform and abolitionist movements could help better illustrate the impacts of racism and classism as the root causes of disproportionality in the system. Finally, interventions can be aimed at implementing policies that require staff training, give young people the right to experience placement without discrimination, or that ensure individuals are housed in appropriate sex-segregated facilities. However, Wilson cautioned, disparities persist even in states with these protections. Thus, there is great value in evaluating existing policies, their implementation and impacts, and the appropriateness of their adaptation across contexts.

PATHS FORWARD IN RESEARCH

To understand the lives and perspectives of youths in the foster care system, Mountz called for "research justice." There is a need to collect data through national systems (e.g., the National Youth in Transition

Database), but there is also a need to "listen beyond the numbers" to the nuanced narratives that young people share about their experiences at the intersection of identities and the interface of systems. This type of research creates opportunities for individual and collective counter-storytelling, harnesses the knowledge of young people, redistributes power, and counters "adultism." As an example, Mountz shared her experiences working on a project called *From Our Perspectives: Untold Stories of LGBTQ Youth in the Los Angeles Foster Care System*. The project used a community-based participatory research (CBPR) approach and was conducted in collaboration with social work students, system-impacted youths, and foster care providers. The stories of 25 LGBTQ former foster youths were told through qualitative interviewing and photo-voice methodology; this culminated in a series of community-based art exhibits attended by over 500 people. The attendees included students, young people, systems-impacted young people and their families, providers, the public, artists, activists, a family court judge, and other scholars; this breadth demonstrates the ability of CBPR approaches to reach people outside of the research community. Mountz shared an example of photo-voice process, in which one participant gave the name "Paper Trail" to a picture of a binder stuffed with paper, and explained that, "I was pretty much a case and I had a long paper trail attached to me, so whenever I moved to group homes they weren't necessarily looking at me as a character or person, they only looked at my paperwork. So, they never asked me what I thought I needed for my healing and process and me trying to get a home." These types of visual approaches can tap into information and experiences that might not otherwise be accessible, and they can help draw the collective experience of a community, Mountz said.

In addition, listening to nuanced narratives can provide information behind the statistics of disproportionate representation. For example, while a common assumption is that the overrepresentation of LGBTQ youth in foster care is due to rejection by their families of origin, only 3 out of 25 study participants identified this as the reason for initial placement in foster care. Instead, participants more frequently referenced parental substance use, mental health issues, poverty, and racism as contributors to their placement in foster care. In addition, participants spoke more often about harms experienced while in the foster care system than about harms stemming from their families of origin. Young people who identify as trans, nonbinary, or gender expansive reported experiencing even greater harms in the system, such as a lack of access to appropriate resources and medical care, and a profound lack of competency among workers and caregivers with regard to gender-affirming language and practices. In addition, these young people experienced twice the rate of placement disruption compared to LGB youth. These narrative data, said Mountz, indicate that, rather than settling into a single narrative, there is a need to expand our understanding to look at the roles of systemic and structural racism and state surveillance, as well as the harms perpetrated by the child protective system itself. This system has created intergenerational family fracture, particularly among communities of color, said Mountz.

Mountz emphasized the importance of researchers giving up some of their power in the research process and partnering with young people. In her experience, members of LGBTQ communities have a strong sense of accountability to their communities and a strong sense of social justice; involving them in research and storytelling is critical for improving our understanding of their experiences and beginning the healing process.

PROMISING INTERVENTIONS

Following the presentations on the landscape of systems research and potential areas for intervention, a panel of speakers presented information about specific interventions to improve the health and well-being of child welfare and juvenile justice system-involved LGBTQ youth.

Juvenile Carceral System Intervention: Youth Justice Agency Policies and Professional Development

Bernadette Brown (B. Brown Consulting) works with juvenile justice agencies to improve the health and well-being of detainees, including LGBTQ youth. Brown's presentation described a model youth justice agency that she worked with to develop policies and procedures pertaining to LGBTQ youth and gender-nonconforming youth, to provide staff training and post-training technical assistance. The agency is in the South, where most young people in detention are youth of color. There is a relatively high number of LGBTQ youth in detention, particularly trans youth. Most of the security staff are people of color and multiple staff members have military backgrounds. Many of the staff also identify as religious. Brown noted that questions pertaining to religion come up frequently in her work, often under the false assumption that cisgender and heterosexual religious adults are anti-LGBTQ.

Her agency faced several immediate challenges, said Brown. First, external stakeholders discouraged her from accepting the project because they thought the work had insufficient support, either within the agency or within the facilities. Second, in certain parts of the state, many LGBTQ youth and their families, particularly youth of color, experienced a lack of external support and community connections. Finally, there was a tremendous amount of political opposition—primarily from the governor—which almost derailed the project before it began. Brown said that she was inspired by the fact that the agency staff banded together to lead the resistance to the governor's opposition.

There were also factors working in favor of the project, said Brown. First, the leader of the initiative within the facility was well respected by his colleagues and was mindful about selecting supportive staff to participate in the effort. Second, the many military veterans on staff were receptive to the changes required by the initiative. Brown said that, while civilian staff sometimes push back against changes, military veteran staff tend to accept the training more readily, viewing it as preparation for fulfilling a new duty. Third, Brown explained that staff were generally open to discussing racism and anti-LGBTQ beliefs and attitudes. Staff members with strong religious beliefs, said Brown, often expect that she will tell them to "put aside all of their beliefs." Instead, Brown emphasizes to staff that her job is not to change their personal beliefs but to help them fulfill their professional responsibilities and obligations. Key successes included the adoption of policies and procedures to support LGBTQ and gender-nonconforming youth in the youth justice agency. Following trainings, staff are also better equipped to locate resources for LGBTQ and gender-nonconforming youth in the community. Trans youths are now regularly assigned to a placement that aligns with their gender identity. Brown said that this change is "highly unusual" and "phenomenal," and is due in part to the commitment of people in leadership roles, including individuals new to leadership roles in the agency.

One unexpected success of her work with this agency, said Brown, was spontaneous youth training on sexual orientation, gender identity, and gender expression. Her planned training was geared toward the adult staff, but a last-minute emergency called most of the staff away. Brown quickly adapted the training to serve a group of youths who were unable to attend their recreation time without available staff. The young people actively participated in the session, which was also attended by a mental health clinician. As a result, the young people felt empowered and became ambassadors for themselves and for the safety of others within their facility. For example, a trans girl had been assigned to a unit for boys and was experiencing harassment and bullying. The trained youths became advocates for this girl and pushed for changes in her treatment and housing. Staff soon realized that making the facility safer for this trans girl also made the facility safer for everyone else and made staff roles easier, said Brown.

Brown identified several actions that are critical for improving the health and well-being of LGBTQ youth in juvenile justice facilities:

- Aligning new LGBTQ-supporting policies and procedures with the core values of the facilities (e.g., the "three C's": care, custody, and control, or the "three S's" of safety, security, and supervision).

- Involving agency counsel in policy development from the beginning to ensure that policies will be implementable.
- Providing training/professional development for staff, even if a policy is not yet in place. Training all types of staff—including security, medical, management, kitchen, and maintenance staff—because every role contributes to the culture of a facility. Partners in other agencies would also benefit from training.
- Providing post-training assistance to support staff who encounter resistance from colleagues when trying to implement new policies.
- Making age-appropriate trainings available for youth. This may require thoughtful explanations to guardians about the role training plays in the overall educational curriculum of the facility.
- Engaging in work to secure appropriate post-detention placements; some youths, particularly trans youths, may end up back in the system because they have no options or support.

Brown noted that partnering with community-based organizations can be a useful approach for improving the well-being of LGBTQ youth in juvenile justice facilities. However, she cautioned that traditional LGBTQ community centers do not typically have a racial justice lens, nor do they generally serve youths who are involved in the juvenile justice system. Instead, she highlighted the importance of helping justice-focused organizations, including faith-based programs, to understand and address sexual orientation, gender identity, and gender expression. Brown emphasized that attendance at LGBTQ community centers should not be a condition of probation; if youths encounter racism and discrimination at a center and choose not to attend, they can be rearrested and detained. Brown encouraged LGBTQ centers to continue to develop a strong racial justice lens and to find ways to support and serve system-involved youths.

Brown concluded her remarks by highlighting key lessons, including the time-intensive nature of cultivating relationships with agencies, the importance of being aware of juvenile corrections staff unions and their views on new policies, and the need for more housing options for youths returning from incarceration.

Child Welfare System: The American Civil Liberties Union of Illinois and the Illinois Department of Children and Family Services

Ghirlandi Guidetti (Legal Aid of Los Angeles) shared the lessons learned from his previous role working on behalf of the American Civil Liberties Union (ACLU) of Illinois, to improve care for LGBTQ youth in custody of the Illinois Department of Children and Family Services (DCFS). DCFS is a statewide system that relies heavily on private contractors, said Guidetti.

In most cases, young people interact almost exclusively with employees of the private contractors. There has been a great deal of instability in the leadership of DCFS, he said, which makes it difficult to implement changes—particularly cultural changes. Guidetti noted that DCFS has, at least on paper, a strong policy regarding the support and well-being of LGBTQ youth. However, the policy is located deep in an appendix of the organization's procedures. Guidetti's work with the ACLU involved both litigation and a collaborative roundtable; he said that the combination of approaches has been effective at improving care for LGBTQ youth in the care of the DCFS.

The ACLU's involvement with DCFS began in 1988, when the ACLU filed a class-action lawsuit. The lawsuit argued that the 14th Amendment rights of youth in care were being violated because DCFS was not protecting children from physical and psychological harm. This lawsuit settled in 1991 with a consent decree, a court-supervised agreement between the ACLU and DCFS. While the case was not LGBTQ specific, said Guidetti, the consent decree gave the ACLU the right to represent all youth in the custody of DCFS, including LGBTQ youth. In 2016, after hearing stories about the experiences of LGBTQ youth in state care, the ACLU asked DCFS to identify the LGBTQ youth in its care. However, DCFS did not have a process for collecting data on sexual orientation, gender identity, or gender expression. Guidetti said that the lack of data collection was driven by fear of misuse of the information but may also have been driven by concern that the data would document known disparities in treatments and outcomes. While information about gender and sexual identity is highly sensitive, said Guidetti, child welfare systems already collect and protect a great deal of other sensitive information about children, such as history of sexual abuse.

The ACLU eventually identified a number of LGBTQ youth by working with community service providers, state contractors, and a statewide LGBTQ specialist. Guidetti reported that, in initial conversations with youths, "virtually none of them" was aware of their rights within the child welfare system. Most youths had experienced discrimination but did not know there was an anti-discrimination policy in place, did not know there was an LGBTQ specialist, and did not know how to contact anyone for help. Guidetti shared examples that he said were illustrative of what they saw in the child welfare system. "Colin" was placed with a foster family and was experiencing bullying from his foster siblings because of his identity. His foster parents took no action, so he reached out to his case worker to report that he felt unsafe. Rather than working with the family or changing the situation, the case worker told him he should feel "lucky" to be in a foster home rather than in congregant care, and suggested that Colin "try to make the best of the situation." Colin later told his case worker that he was suicidal, knowing that this would result in his removal from the foster home. He ended up in a psychiatric hospital and was kept there beyond the period of medical necessity. Trans youth in the system reported that medically appropriate care was often delayed as a result of DCFS holding up necessary medical consents and processes, and medical advisors and therapists used by DCFS often did not have the experience or qualifications to treat trans youth, said Guidetti. He relayed the story of a youth in care who began questioning their gender identity at 12 years old. As a result, their favorite staff person at their residential facility started treating them differently, and this had a negative impact on the youth.

Guidetti identified several lessons learned from his experience with the ACLU lawsuit and the work that followed. First, he suggested that collecting data on sexual orientation, gender identity, and gender expression is critical for enforcement of nondiscrimination policies, for protecting youth, and for comparing outcomes against non-LGBTQ peers. LGBTQ youth cannot be protected if no one knows who they are, and every young person who comes out deserves a safe and affirming placement, said Guidetti. On the system level, disparities cannot be addressed unless data are collected and sorted by LGBTQ identity. The second lesson, he said, is that youth voices are powerful drivers of change. As part of its advocacy work, the ACLU shared stories of LGBTQ youth in care with administrators, legislative partners, and other stakeholders; one direct result was a legislative resolution calling for a performance audit of DCFS's care of LGBTQ youth. The resulting report was released in February 2021 and gave DCFS a failing grade.

Guidetti shifted gears to discuss his work on the Illinois LGBTQ Roundtable. The Roundtable is a coalition of DCFS-contracted providers, LGBTQ advocates, and child welfare advocates. Their priority issues include:

- Mandatory training of DCFS, service providers, and foster families;
- Meaningful implementation of the anti-discrimination policy (i.e., "Appendix K");
- Data collection on sexual orientation, gender identity, and gender expression;
- Matching of LGBTQ youth with affirming placements; and
- Allocation of resources to adequately address the needs of youth in care.

Many of these actions are under development and being implemented soon, said Guidetti. Training has been a challenge—DCFS originally developed its own content in-house, but other stakeholders found training content to be inadequate. New content was developed with the help of a subject-matter expert. Data collection will begin shortly and was expedited by an Illinois legislative mandate that requires all state agencies to collect information on gender and sexual identity. A "Chief of LGBTQI Services" position is being created within the Office of Affirmative Action, which will allow collaboration across departments to ensure system-wide changes and policy implementation. In addition, DCFS is establishing an LGBTQ Youth Advisory Board, which Guidetti said is the direct result of decision makers realizing the importance of listening to the stories and perspectives of young people in the system.

Child Welfare System: National Quality Improvement Center

Angela Weeks (University of Maryland School of Social Work) presented her work with The National Quality Improvement Center on Tailored Services, Placement Stability, and Permanency for Lesbian, Gay, Bisexual, Transgender, Questioning, and Two-Spirit Children and Youth in Foster Care. This was a 5-year project designed to build the evidence base for LGBTQ youth and family programming, with the specific purpose of increasing stability, increasing permanency, and improving well-being. When the program started, Weeks said, there was a lack of data about the types of programming useful for this population. Many programs did not have written documents describing their design or practices, so one of the Center's goals was to develop programs that could be replicated on a wide scale. Over the course of 5 years, the Center worked with partners to implement a number of interventions, including staff and caregiver training, data collection, and clinical interventions for families and young people. At the outset of the work, some projects were already developed, others were in development, and many did not yet exist. Now, said Weeks, nearly all of their interventions have been implemented and evaluated.

Weeks shared the lessons learned from her experiences with the Center. Many interventions, she said, begin with LGBTQ-focused trainings for staff. These trainings often focus on changing knowledge, attitudes, and behavior. The evaluations conducted by the Center found that, while training could initially produce changes in all three areas, most people reverted to their previous attitudes and behaviors within 3 months of training. Weeks said that this evidence suggests that an "annual booster" approach to training may not be sufficient, and that quick follow-up after initial training may be necessary. The next set of lessons centered around the differences between group and individual clinical interventions. Group interventions were 2-hour sessions, held weekly for 8 weeks, with a clinician and a group of people discussing a topic. These sessions had higher rates of participation, engagement, and graduation; Weeks hypothesized that this was due in part to the interventions having set start and end dates, which people felt they could commit to. In addition, the group setting may have been less stigmatizing for attendees. However, she said, the group sessions were not the best intervention for families who were struggling with a child's sexual orientation or gender identity. Weeks and her team found that individual interventions were most successful when they were conducted before the child was removed from the home, and Weeks emphasized that prevention is key to helping families and youths navigate conflict over gender and sexual identity. The third lesson was that there are no impossible families. Weeks said that staff often believe that certain families—because of their beliefs, culture, or personal biases—will never make the changes necessary to accept and support their children. This is an area in which a paradigm shift is needed, said Weeks. In fact, she explained, all families are capable of change if they can engage in the right intervention at the right dosage. What often happens, she said, is that agencies do not have the necessary programs in place or staff do not have the necessary resources, skills, and tools needed to help a family. Rather than recognizing this gap, service providers may instead label a family as "impossible."

The final lesson from Weeks' work is that staff discomfort can present a key challenge to collecting data on sexual orientation, gender identity, and gender expression. She noted that, while child welfare staff often ask very personal questions of young people and their families, conversations around sex and gender are new and staff require support to incorporate these questions into their work. In addition, she said, it can be helpful for staff to have the ability to refer young people to appropriate programs or resources in direct response to information collected about sexual and gender identity. This can help staff feel that there is a purpose in asking these sensitive questions. As an example of a successful multilevel intervention strategy, Weeks described a systems-change effort in Cuyahoga County, Ohio, focused on implementing the collection of sexual orientation and gender identity and expression (SOGIE) data in child welfare systems. The program developed a three-phased approach to training that became more in-depth over time and incorporated intensive, educational coaching and supervision. The program provided staff with scripts and held sessions during which staff could role-play and practice conversations. They also developed methods for reporting SOGIE information in ways that were as confidential as possible while still informing and improving the allocation of resources. In addition, said Weeks, the program incorporated innovative ideas that were informed by the youths in its care, for example, a pronoun campaign. Through this integrated and comprehensive approach, she said, the issue of supporting LGBTQ youth was consistently present in the minds of staff. Weeks noted that the success of this program is demonstrated by the increase of young people in this foster program's care who openly identify as LGBTQ.

REFLECTIONS

Following the panelist presentations, planning committee member Aisha Canfield (Ceres Policy Research) led a question-and-answer session with panelists. Workshop audience members were also invited to submit questions for panelists via the virtual livestream. Canfield started by asking the speakers to dream with her about a world in which liberation is the model system. Given the ongoing discussions about abolishing police, closing youth detention centers, and ending foster care as we know it, she asked speakers to discuss the opportunities and drawbacks for LGBTQ youth of color in the interventions highlighted by the panelists. Canfield emphasized the importance of contextualizing this work in the current political climate and allowing young advocates to set the tone for future work in the field. Weeks responded by saying that, in her project, most of the youths are Black and most of the workforce is White, which creates dynamics that require careful attention and navigation. The National Quality Improvement Center, Weeks explained, works within the current framework to improve the foster care system and reduce harm, rather than working to dismantle the system itself. Weeks noted that it can be difficult to strike the correct balance between trying to improve the current system through interventions and getting out of the system entirely, and that her team constantly grapples with this challenge. Guidetti concurred with this tension, noting that he often wonders if he is reinforcing the system in a way that will make abolition more difficult. Weeks added that, early in the pandemic foster care agencies were forced to shift to virtual services. Communities of color reported feeling relief at the reduced presence of foster care system staff in their neighborhoods, as well as relief in the absence of unsolicited in-person visits. Brown said that this topic comes up often in her work, and she believes the ability to create profit through incarceration must be eliminated. She suggested that when a region's economic security and viability are based on incarceration, it is enormously difficult to change. Brown urged people to begin the change process by engaging with corporations and individuals that are profiting from the carceral system.

A workshop participant asked speakers to comment on how to get agencies to incorporate mandatory and consistent professional development for supporting LGBTQ youth. Guidetti responded that there are often hard-working advocates within the foster care system who do not have the authority or the resources necessary to make such changes; assisting these people and creating outside pressure on the agencies to support them is critical for change. Weeks noted that some of her sites used anonymous surveys to give leadership and staff information about situations occurring in their programs. Reports from young people detailing how they were treated had a much greater impact on staff than did data from outside studies, and this information helped build traction and buy-in.

During their presentations, several speakers discussed how the structures of the systems they work in contribute to the marginalization of LGBTQ youth. Canfield asked the speakers whether these deficits were due to a lack of resources or a lack of political will. Brown responded that resource issues *are* a matter of political will. "When people want to get stuff done, they get it done," and when they do not, they generate reasons why they cannot, she explained. Guidetti agreed and said that, despite living in a state with an anti-discrimination policy in place, a pro-LGBTQ governor, and DCFS directors who support LGBTQ initiatives, "there is a lot of lip service but not a lot of action." Weeks observed that some of the difficulty stems from the fact that foster care systems were not built to protect and serve people, but rather to police families. Making structural changes to the system itself is an overwhelming and difficult process, but Weeks expressed gratitude that some agencies are engaging in this work.

Another workshop participant noted that Latinx and Black girls in the child welfare and juvenile justice systems are at high risk of multiple negative outcomes and these disparities persist into adulthood; the participant asked speakers to comment on the unique factors that may increase these risks. Weeks responded that the intersection of multiple systems of oppression plays a key role in these outcomes. Latinx and Black girls experience sexism, racism, and anti-LGBTQ biases, while navigating child welfare and juvenile justice systems that were built for cisgender, heterosexual boys. In addition, there is an extreme lack of services for this population, she said. Weeks suggested the need for more culturally adaptive programs that meet the specific needs of Latinx and Black girls, but that there is not enough research to support evidence-based development of such programs. Brown added that Latinx and Black LGBTQ girls are often held to cultural norms involving how girls should behave and dress, and that society also "adultifies" these girls at young ages (i.e., views them as less innocent than their White peers). Brown concluded her comments by highlighting the importance of trainings and laws to counter the role of misogyny and racism in shaping the treatment of child welfare and juvenile justice system-involved sexual- and gender-minority Latinx and Black girls.

4

Promising Interventions for Families and Communities

On the second day of the workshop, speakers and participants discussed how families and communities influence the health and well-being of LGBTQ youth and identified promising interventions in this area.

RESEARCH LANDSCAPE: OUTCOMES AND KNOWN INTERVENTIONS

LGBTQ youth are a dynamic and phenomenal group of people, said J. Garrett-Walker (University of Toronto); however, they live in a world that has many systems and structures in place that seek to oppress them. When compared to heterosexual peers, LGBTQ youth have higher rates of mood and anxiety disorders, higher risk of homelessness and food insecurity, and higher rates of suicidal ideation and victimization. These differences, said Garrett-Walker, are "solely due to the oppressive world in which they live." Given that these disparities exist, she asked, what can be done about it? Family is critical in the development of a healthy psychosocial identity, she said, and family support allows LGBTQ youth to "live in their truth." There are interventions that can improve a family's ability to support and communicate with their child. For example, an online intervention has been developed to help families of trans children find the proper language to use, and it teaches them about key challenges facing their children (Sharek et al., 2021). Another online program offers resources including educational videos, videos of trans youth and their parents, and writing activities; focus groups examining this program reported positive feedback on the helpfulness of the program for participants (Matsuno and Israel, 2021). In addition to families, communities can be enormously impactful in young people's lives. A 2019 study found that young people who engaged with queer-focused, community-based organizations reported less substance use, and consistent participation in these organizations was associated with higher self-esteem (Fish et al., 2019). Neighborhoods, religious communities, and community-based organizations can support LGBTQ youth, or they can serve as a source of marginalization and oppression, said Garrett-Walker. To serve and support queer youth, we must seek to understand the nuanced experiences they have in their various communities, she said.

PROMISING INTERVENTIONS

In this session of the workshop, a panel of speakers presented information about family- and community-based interventions to improve the health and well-being of LGBTQ youth.

Family Interventions: Lead with Love and PATHS

There are decades of research on the powerful influence that parents have on adolescent health, said David Huebner (George Washington University School of Public Health). Regardless of sexual orientation or gender identity, the quality of parent-child attachment, parent monitoring, and parent-child communication impacts a child's health and well-being. In addition, there is emerging research documenting the impact of parent behaviors in the LGBTQ context, including research on rejection and acceptance of a child's sexual- and gender-minority (SGM) status, support for gender-affirming treatments, and communication about HIV and other illnesses. Despite this evidence base, said Huebner, interventions to address these influences are extremely limited. Support groups such as PFLAG[1] have been offering support to parents for decades, but there is little empirical research that examines whether and how these interventions work. Clinical intervention models (e.g., trauma-focused cognitive behavioral therapy (CBT)) have been described by scholars but also lack empirical support. Huebner noted that researchers have recently begun to explore how interventions developed for the general population can be used in the LGBTQ population, including one study on sexual risk behaviors among gay and bisexual boys that reported positive results (Ocasio et al., 2021). There are a few interventions for parents of SGM youth that have some empirical evaluation, said Huebner; he identified four that he is aware of:

---

[1] In 2014, the organization officially changed its name from "Parents, Families, and Friends of Lesbians and Gays" to simply "PFLAG."

1. Attachment-based family therapy (Diamond et al., 2012);
2. Lead with Love (Huebner et al., 2013);
3. Parent Resource for Increasing Sexual Minority Support (PRISMS) (Goodman and Israel, 2020); and
4. https://www.avawomen.com/avaworld/how-long-to-get-pregnant.

Before delving into the details of interventions, Huebner described the foundational premises of his work on interventions with parents of SGM youth. First, his work is based on the premise that parent behaviors are powerful predictors of the health of SGM youth and therefore intervening to change parent behavior is one approach to improving children's health. Second, parents of SGM youth are fundamentally concerned about their children's health and well-being even if they are expressing rejection. Huebner suggested that rejection is often a misguided expression of parental concern, and that even those parents who are not accepting of their child's SGM status are often motivated to support their child's health. The third foundational premise is that interventions need to reach parents where they are, both geographically and emotionally. Huebner's research found that 85–90 percent of parents of SGM youth never attend any type of therapy or support group. Based on these premises, Huebner and his colleagues have developed two parent-focused interventions: Lead with Love and Parents and Adolescents Talking about Healthy Sexuality.

Lead with Love

Lead with Love is a film-based intervention designed to support parents, decrease parent rejection, and increase positive parenting behaviors (Huebner et al., 2013). The 35-minute film is documentary style; Huebner said this genre of education entertainment has been effectively used to change many types of behaviors. The film, which is available for free online,[2] was accompanied by a multimedia promotion campaign upon its release. The film uses principles of motivational interviewing and stage-based theories of change. Huebner explained that the first goal in creating this intervention was to make parents feel "understood in their distress." The second goal was to make parents aware that their distress is not because there is something inherently wrong with being gay, but because of a deep concern about their child's well-being and a misunderstanding of what it means to be a sexual minority. The third goal was improving parents' knowledge about sexual orientation (e.g., that it is not an illness and that it cannot be changed). Stories from parents and children are used to increase parents' motivation to change their behavior; the stories discuss

---

[2] See www.leadwithlovefilm.com.

the negative impacts that parental rejection can have and the importance of parental love and understanding to a child's well-being. The film also provides specific behavioral guidance to parents. The guidance encourages parents to "LEAD" with love:

- Let your affection show;
- Express your pain away from your child;
- Avoid rejecting behaviors; and
- Do good before you feel good.

The film was primarily evaluated through process data, said Huebner. In the first year, it reached 1,800 parents of LGB youth from 48 states. Of these parents, 21 percent had known about their child's LGB status for less than a month, and 36 percent said having an LGB child was extremely or very hard for them. These data, said Huebner, indicate that the film is not just reaching the "worried well," but is reaching parents who really need support. According to their evaluations, most parents found the film helpful, and there were significant increases in parents' feeling of self-efficacy for parenting an LGB child. Fully 86 percent of parents who viewed the film had never accessed any other intervention or support. Huebner relayed a story about one family that accessed the film through a DVD order. Their home was in a tiny border town surrounded by cotton fields. Huebner noted that there are likely no PFLAG chapters or therapists equipped to provide LGBTQ-affirming care in this and other low-population areas. This highlights the need, said Huebner, for interventions that can reach families in every inhabited corner of the world.

Parents and Adolescents Talking about Healthy Sexuality

The second intervention developed by Huebner and his colleagues is called Parents and Adolescents Talking about Healthy Sexuality (PATHS) (Huebner et al., 2021). The ultimate goal of this intervention is to reduce HIV-related sexual risk behaviors among gay and bisexual adolescent boys. Huebner said the intervention seeks to accomplish this by targeting parent behaviors that are shown to be supportive of adolescent sexual health: communicating with their sons about HIV, instructing their sons on the mechanics of condom use, facilitating their sons' access to condoms, and helping their sons get HIV tests. The intervention is based on the integrated behavior model and is aimed at increasing parents' self-efficacy to support their children's sexual health, improving attitudes, reducing barriers around parent support for adolescent sexual health, and changing parents' expectations about the consequences of talking about sex. PATHS is delivered through an online application that includes videos of parents and adolescent health experts, animated clips, and goal-setting activities. Huebner and his colleagues conducted a randomized, controlled trial to evaluate this intervention, with 61 ethnically diverse parent-child dyads, and found that the program significantly increased both parent and child reports of how much information parents shared about HIV, how much instruction they provided about condom use, and how much facilitated their sons' access to condoms. In addition, families in the intervention group reported that their children were more likely to get tested for HIV in the 3 months following the intervention.

In closing, Huebner identified several challenges and needs in this area. There is a need for intervention models that can reach people where they are, geographically and emotionally, and that are appropriate for diverse families (e.g., across differences in ethnicity, family composition, and religion). Huebner said that the needs of gender-diverse youth need to be addressed, though these young people may need interventions different from those designed for sexual minority youth. He noted that there are almost no interventions for parents of gender-diverse youth that have any empirical support, and he encouraged the development of complementary interventions to address the needs of LGB youth and gender-diverse youth. Huebner also stated that parent-focused interventions need to be designed not only to increase general parent acceptance, but also to help parents engage in the specific behaviors that are likely to have an impact on the health risks that SGM youth disproportionately face. In conclusion, Huebner suggested that future interventions need to be described thoroughly to enable dissemination and replication, and that efforts to accurately measure the efficacy of those interventions would benefit greatly from rigorous evaluation.

Community Intervention: Community Centers and CenterLink

LGBTQ community centers provide incredible prevention and intervention services to youths, said Deborah Levine (CenterLink). CenterLink supports, strengthens, and connects a network of over 270 LGBTQ centers, 83 percent of which have a youth program or exclusively serve youths. Levine began her presentation by describing in general terms what these centers do and who they serve. She noted that centers are highly responsive to youths; a survey showed that youth demand is the most important factor in deciding which services to offer, and many centers have formal or informal youth leadership programs. Providing general support and activities is a main function of these centers. For example, many have drop-in spaces with TVs, art supplies, snacks, and comfortable seating, and hold gatherings such as support groups, educational programs, movie nights, and proms. Even if a youth cannot attend the center often, said Levine, just the knowledge that it exists can be a support. Centers also provide social services, including mental health counseling, family support, STD testing, healthcare, and access to computers, meals, clothing, laundry services, and showers; centers may also refer youths to other agencies to serve needs not met by the center. The staff at these centers also advocate for LGBTQ youth in the community, by providing professional development for teachers, counselors, and healthcare providers; providing consultation advocacy at the system level; and initiating and supporting GSAs—student-based support groups bringing LGBTQ+ and allied youth together to build community—in local schools. Levine noted that many centers have few staff members, and nearly one-quarter of CenterLink centers are entirely volunteer run. Since the beginning of the COVID-19 pandemic, many of these services and support mechanisms have been conducted virtually (see Box 4-1).

BOX 4-1
Digital Tools for Support

Digital programming is an important mechanism for supporting LGBTQ youth, said Levine. Even before the pandemic, many LGBTQ youth were unable to access in-person services due to geography, transportation, unsupportive parents, anxiety, or other factors. Levine described some digital tools currently in use. Q Chat Space was developed by CenterLink, PFLAG, and Planned Parenthood; it provides anonymous, facilitated chat-based support discussions for LGBTQ teens. This model replicates support groups, which are the service most commonly provided to youths at centers. Q Chat users have reported that it has been life changing, helping them to find friends and community, and easing anxiety, said Levine. HopeLab is currently developing a digital tool that will be distributed by CenterLink to complement Q Chat. This new tool will use science-backed methods to help youths explore topics related to their queer identities and experiences. Other digital programs include:

- Trevor Space, a social networking site for LGBTQ youth;
- Gender Spectrum, online support groups for trans and gender-diverse youth;
- Roo, an AI-powered chat bot that answers questions about sexual health and relationships;
- OkaySo, an app that connects young people to vetted experts who provide personalized support and information; and
- RealTalk, an app that crowd-sources and curates authentic stories from teens.

While some of these tools are not specific to LGBTQ youth, in her work Levine has found that LGBTQ youth are overrepresented in the community of users. Levine said that this demonstrates that digital tools are needed for this population, and that youths are likely to engage with them.

The services offered by LGBTQ centers are not particularly innovative, said Levine. What makes these centers work is "the village" of adults who are looking out for youths, helping to smooth the transition to adulthood, remedying the hurts that youths experience, and advocating to prevent future harm. Unfortunately, there is a lack of research to document the impact of this community work, she said. Levine argued that there is a critical need for researchers to engage with community centers, to compensate participants for their time, and to have clear plans for disseminating the results in the community. Positive results from such research could be used to encourage funders to support the growth of LGBTQ youth programs, Levine said.

Even with the lack of data, community-based LGBTQ youth support programs are being scaled up and replicated. People in communities—from hairdressers to woodworkers—have stepped up to develop youth programs. Organizations such as libraries, churches, and recreation departments can implement programs in their communities. The primary challenge to scaling up, said Levine, is funding. A secondary challenge is providing the appropriate training and education for those who want to do the work. People who are part of the LGBTQ community need training on working with young people, and people who work with youths need training on working with LGBTQ youth. Those already in the field need professional development to ensure that their work continues to have the intended impact. For example, centers are reporting an increase in gender-diverse youth, youth of color, and younger youth, so staff may require specialized training and resources to appropriately serve these populations. Levine stressed the importance of finding ways to serve youths who experience other intersecting inequities, for example, LGBTQ youth of color. Almost half of CenterLink's programs serve primarily youth of color, and these centers are more likely than others to provide key social services such as educational programs, job placement, and transitional housing. As the community center model is scaled, she said, it is essential that communities of color have the resources and staff necessary to "be the village" for LGBTQ youth of color.

Community Intervention: Rainbow Pride Youth Alliance

Rainbow Pride Youth Alliance (RPYA) was formed in 2001 when "a group of LGBTQ Black, Indigenous, people of color (BIPOC) youth showed up to a gathering of mostly white, cisgender LGBT adults and said, 'We need a safe space to be,'" said Reverend Benita Ramsey (Rainbow Pride Youth Alliance). RPYA is volunteer led and serves youths ages 12–26 in the Inland Empire area of California. Its mission is to "provide a safe, healthy, and enriching environment for LGBTQI youth to grow." RPYA offers comprehensive services that promote the well-being and empowerment of

LGBTQ youth, using a social justice development framework that centers around youth perspectives and amplifies youth voices. Ramsey explained that youth voices guide the programming, pedagogy, and organizational structure of RPYA, and from the program's inception youths have been equally positioned as governing board members.

RPYA offers weekly support groups using a proven model that positions 1 hour of educational time between 2 hours of social time, said Ramsey. Other services include art and wellness workshops, GSA support, and youth leadership development. RPYA also works to support youth engagement and leadership in schools and faith communities. The staff of RPYA reflects the diversity of the community, said Ramsey; they "live, work, play, and attend spiritual services" in the area, are familiar with neighborhood histories, and have established relationships with key "cultural brokers."

Ramsey's presentation also highlighted the Pride Youth Leadership and Resiliency Project, a school- and community-based program for LGBTQ youth that was adapted from the Fairfax Resiliency Prevention strategy. The program is aimed at preventing substance use and justice-system involvement by improving resiliency in three areas: healthy relationships, goal setting, and coping strategies. There are five main areas of activities in the program, noted Ramsey. First is a weekly resiliency group that builds social competencies and includes discussions on topics such as substance use, peer refusal skills, oppression, and spirituality. The second activity uses the creative and performing arts to strengthen protective factors. In this activity, youths create "classrooms" to depict a typical day for LGBTQ youth who face bullying, harassment, and the pressure to use substances. Parents, educators, service providers, and elected officials are invited to attend, and after each performance the youths facilitate community dialogue to discuss ideas for change. These performances serve both to recruit new participants and to provide participants the opportunity reframe their cognitive perceptions and develop shared norms, said Ramsey. The third activity is service learning, which helps to create school and community bonds and to build relationships with positive role models and other caring adults. Activity four is monthly adventures such as hiking and fishing. These adventures allow youths to gain experiences in positive risk taking and decision making, which can lead to increased self-reliance, coping skills, and the ability to manage risks in day-to-day life. Finally, said Ramsey, the program includes a youth-led digital network designed to educate parents and caregivers on LGBTQ history, with information on the school-to-prison pipeline, the war on drugs, and laws that protect LGBTQ youth.

Young people have great insights and ideas, said Ramsey, and they should be included as active partners in developing strategies to improve their own health and the social conditions of their lives. She emphasized the value of creating opportunities for youths to lead, not to simply have a seat at the table. The active participation and leadership of young people can help ensure that culturally responsive, affirming, trauma-informed prevention and treatment services are available to all youth who need them. Brown also called attention to the importance of funders and programs creating opportunities for LGBTQ youth of color to be compensated for the time and energy they put into these programs. In short, she said, "let [youth] speak; their voices change hearts and minds."

REFLECTIONS

Following the panelist presentations, planning committee member Jama Shelton (Hunter College) led a discussion session with panelists. Workshop audience members were also invited to submit questions for panelists via the virtual livestream. Shelton began by asking panelists to think about who is *not* at the table but could be an integral part of reducing inequities for LGBTQ young people. Levine responded that parents are an untapped resource. LGBTQ community centers were founded at a time when there was an assumption that most parents would not be involved in supporting LGBTQ children, she said, and this paradigm is shifting quickly. Parental involvement at centers should be encouraged, and trusted community allies (e.g., faith leaders) could be used to connect with parents who may be reluctant to work with centers directly. Ramsey added that LGBTQ people who are parents are sometimes overlooked; these individuals and their children bring a unique perspective to the table, and they can be compassionate partners when working with other parents. In addition, she said, foster parents and other caregivers need support and training, and are welcome at RPYA's parent services. Huebner noted the need to better engage with faith partners across the spectrum. He said that it is possible to find common ground and to make progress even in churches that do not explicitly embrace the LGBTQ community. Ramsey concurred and said that they engage with faith leaders on issues like homelessness and food insecurity, and from there "we are able to navigate some of the stickier conversations around the needs of LGBT youth." Ramsey reemphasized the importance of youth sharing their voices and elevating their stories to reach nontraditional partners.

A workshop participant followed up on Levine's response to ask how centers engage with parents and families. Levine answered that one common strategy is to hold support meetings for youths and parents that are separate but simultaneous. She described one center that does not hold a formal group for the parents but serves coffee while the parents are waiting for their children—the parents are essentially attending a support group, but it has the feeling of an informal, organic gathering. In addition, centers often conduct trainings in the communities where parents are gathering, for example, at Parent Teacher Association meetings and through faith-based organizations. Another common way that centers engage with parents, said Levine, is through advocacy for an individual student; for example, by helping a family navigate a gender transition in the school system. Huebner added that, in his experience, parents want to engage in "all of the spaces that their kids are spending time in," from schools to swim teams to LGBTQ youth centers. He agreed that there has been a major shift away from the idea that parents are the "enemy" and he encouraged centers to find ways to include all parents, even those who lack the time or ability to volunteer.

Shelton asked speakers to comment on the role of "chosen family" in providing support for young people in the LGBTQ community. Ramsey replied that it is very common for young people who are not accepted at home to create a network of chosen family. This is one of the reasons, she said, that her organization offers adult-youth experiences to build relationships. Levine said that LGBTQ centers use explicit conversations about chosen family as a way to orient young people to the LGBTQ community and to encourage them to proactively build a supportive network. Even when a child's family of origin is supportive, it can be helpful to have a chosen family within the community, she said. For youths who are unstably housed, some centers coordinate "host homes," where supportive adults are assisted by the centers in offering space to young people.

Another workshop participant asked about the role of LGBTQ elders and intergenerational connections to help support LGBTQ youth. Levine responded that a number of centers have LGBTQ elders as volunteers, and described one center that mixes seniors with young people for job training. However, much of the work in this area is informal, and Levine said it would be useful to have a more formal understanding of how to develop and support intergenerational relationships. Huebner added that, when considering new programs like this, it is important to consider existing programs outside of the LGBTQ space that could be adapted for the community. "We don't need to reinvent the wheel every time," he said.

5

Promising Interventions in Mental, Emotional, and Physical Health

On the third day of the workshop, speakers and participants discussed the mental, emotional, and physical health of LGBTQ youth and identified promising interventions in these areas.

LANDSCAPE: OUTCOMES, INEQUALITIES, AND KNOWN INTERVENTIONS

The health disparities between LGBTQ youth and their cisgender, heterosexual peers are well documented, said Margaret Rosario (The Graduate Center, CUNY). However, there are interventions that can help reduce these disparities and allow LGBTQ youth to develop their sexual and gender identities in a safe, supportive environment, she said. One approach for improving the health of LGBTQ youth is increasing positive societal attitudes toward sexual-minority and gender-diverse individuals. Empirical data support this approach, said Rosario. Positive attitudes toward LGBTQ individuals steadily increased between 1988 and 2014, and after the Supreme Court ruled in favor of same-sex marriage in *Obergefell v. Hodges* in 2015, positive attitudes increased dramatically. Other drivers of the increase in positive attitudes include increasing contact with LGB individuals, decreasing religiosity, and increasing education. These attitudes are related to health outcomes among both heterosexuals and LGBTQ individuals. For example, in communities with more positive attitudes toward gay marriage, LGBTQ individuals are less likely to smoke or to report poor or fair health. In states that passed constitutional bans against gay marriage prior to *Obergefell*, LGB individuals experienced an increase in psychiatric morbidity once the ban was in place. LGB individuals living in states without a gay marriage ban had no change in psychiatric morbidity, said Rosario. Finally, she said, negative attitudes toward "homosexuality" are related to higher mortality among heterosexual individuals.

There are, of course, more direct interventions for improving the health of LGBTQ youth, said Rosario. These include interventions in school settings (see Chapter 6), interventions with parents (see Chapter 4), and interventions designed to educate, support, and affirm LGBTQ youth. This chapter focuses on how these types of interventions can improve mental and physical health in the LGBTQ community and reduce disparities between these youths and their cisgender, heterosexual peers.

In his day-one presentation, Jose Bauermeister offered several suggestions for future research on the mental and physical health of LGBTQ youth. First, he highlighted the value of involving youths as appraisers of systems and services. Bauermeister developed a project in which young people from the LGBTQ community acted as mystery shoppers for HIV testing and counseling services and graded the services based on their experiences (Bauermeister et al., 2019). He suggested that, rather than placing the onus for change on youth, we should focus on ensuring that existing systems are operating at their highest levels. Second, developmental theory should be integrated into interventions for sexual- and gender-minority (SGM) youth, according to Bauermeister. For example, the IREACH app contains developmental content across 16 life-skill domains, including goal-setting activities. Third, he noted the need for interventions that are culturally relevant and that address geospatial variations, including the wide variation in access to LGBTQ-affirming providers across the country. Fourth, Bauermeister offered a word of warning about the use of technology and reminded the audience that building an app is not enough to create behavioral changes. Impactful technology must be integrated with the lived reality of young people and with the availability of trained providers, particularly if the technology is encouraging youths to receive services. Finally, he emphasized that his team's interventions are created "for, by, and with youth." He noted the crucial importance of programs that include opportunities for youths to participate and engage, particularly youth of color. Youths can help think about problems, think about solutions, implement solutions, and help ensure that interventions are used in the "real world," outside of clinical trials.

PROMISING INTERVENTIONS

In this session of the workshop, a panel of speakers presented information about interventions that are designed improve the mental, emotional, and physical health and well-being of LGBTQ youth.

Mental Health Interventions: EQuIP

John Pachankis (Yale School of Public Health) began his presentation by pointing out the substantial mental health inequities facing LGBTQ youth. Sexual- and gender-minority youth are at greater risk for depressive disorder, post-traumatic stress disorder, lifetime mental disorders, suicidal ideation, and suicide attempts than are their cisgender, heterosexual peers (Clark et al., 2020; Johns et al., 2020; Lipson et al., 2019; Day, et al., 2017). These mental health inequalities begin early in life, said Pachankis, with disparities in depression becoming significantly pronounced by middle school (Pachankis et al., 2021). The most studied sources of these disparities are structural stigma, bullying, and family rejection, said Pachankis. Structural stigma include laws and policies that do not support LGBTQ youth (e.g., bathroom bills, lack of bans on conversion therapy, and lack of anti-bullying policies). Associations between mental health disparities and structural stigma, bullying, and family rejection have been found in population-based, prospective, longitudinal studies (Clark et al., 2020; la Roi et al., 2016; Hatzenbuehler et al., 2015a). These upstream factors, said Pachankis, could serve as promising intervention targets. For example, sexual-minority youth in school districts with anti-bullying policies have a lower likelihood of attempting suicide (Meyer et al., 2019; Hatzenbuehler et al., 2015b, 2014). The data are less clear on the association between mental health and conversion therapy bans (Turban et al., 2020; Ryan et al., 2018) and bathroom access (Horne et al., 2021; Murchison et al., 2019). Some interventions addressing bullying have been evaluated, but few were randomized trials, and few specifically examined the impact of these interventions on SGM mental health (Poteat et al., 2020; Earnshaw et al., 2018; NASEM, 2016; Espelage et al., 2015). Although parental rejection is one of the most prominent sources of SGM mental health disparities, Pachankis noted the lack of widely disseminated and evaluated parenting interventions. Huebner noted that psychotherapy and psychoeducational interventions have shown promise in this area (Goodman and Israel, 2020; Huebner et al., 2013; Diamond et al., 2012; Ryan et al., 2010).

Interventions targeted at changing the stressors associated with poor mental health are one approach to improving LGBTQ mental health, said Pachankis; another approach is changing how SGM youth react to these stressors. For example, stressors like structural stigma are associated with stress adaptations including identity concealment, internalized stigma, and social isolation, all of which are associated with poorer mental health (Pachankis et al., 2020a; Hatzenbuehler, 2009; Meyer, 2003). Pachankis explained that because these reactions are cognitive, affective, and behavioral, they can be addressed through mental health services. There are a number of mental health services available to LGBTQ youth, some of which have been shown to be promising, he said. Crisis services, like those provided by The Trevor Project, offer support via phone, chat, or text (see below). A 2017 evaluation found that youths found the service supportive and would seek it again, and for over 90 percent of respondents, it de-escalated suicidality (The Trevor Project, 2017). Online support groups, such as Q Chat Space, offer live chat for support and community building in noncrisis times, and youths have reported positive experiences with this modality (Fish et al., 2021). There are online cognitive behavioral therapy (CBT) games (e.g., Rainbow Sparx) that showed promising results for reducing psychological symptoms in a small pilot study (Lucassen et al., 2015). Finally, said Pachankis, group CBT therapy has been evaluated, and one intervention called AFFIRM showed promise in reducing depression and building coping skills (Craig et al., 2021; see below). However, none of these interventions has been tested in a randomized controlled trial (RCT). Pachankis explained that RCTs are important for ruling out confounding factors and for comparing the efficacy of various interventions, and he noted that this is an important area for future research.

Pachankis shared the results of his work evaluating the efficacy of LGBTQ-affirmative CBT. One intervention, Empowering Queer Identities in Psychotherapy (EQuIP), specifically addresses an individual's reactions to stressors. It is delivered in 10 one-on-one sessions; the therapist helps the young person become aware of potential stressors, overcome engrained emotion-avoidance patterns such as drinking or self-harm, learn effective communication skills, rework the internalization of anti-LGBTQ messages, and build a supportive community. Two waitlist-controlled trials found that the treatment worked significantly better than the waitlist in terms of improving mental health outcomes for both sexual-minority men and SGM young women (Pachankis, 2020b, 2015). Pachankis and colleagues (2021b) also conducted the only known RCT comparing an LGBTQ-affirmative mental health intervention to an active control. In a population of 254 young gay and bisexual men, the study compared EQuIP to a single session of community-delivered HIV testing and counseling. EQuIP was comparatively more efficacious at reducing measures of depression, suicidality, anxiety, substance use, alcohol abuse, and HIV risk transmission behavior. One of the most robust findings from these studies, said Pachankis, is that LGBTQ-affirmative CBT is more efficacious than existing mental health treatments for Black, Latinx, and Asian participants compared to White participants (Keefe et al., 2021). Pachankis said these results suggest that a focus on stressors may have particular benefit for young men of color, perhaps due to their experiences of racial and minority stressors.

While it is concerning that mental health interventions are not as advanced as they could be, Pachankis concluded, this gap presents enormous opportunity for the future. Pachankis identified several questions that future research could address:

- How are LGBTQ youth already supporting their mental health and building resilience?
- How can LGBTQ-affirmative mental health services best address the needs of transgender youth and LGBTQ youth of color?
- Are existing LGBTQ-affirmative mental health services efficacious?
- How can we best match LGBTQ youth to proper treatment approaches?
- How can effective LGBTQ-affirmative models be implemented widely and efficiently?

Pachankis said that research addressing these questions is needed to better utilize limited mental health resources and to address the specific mental health needs of LGBTQ youth. For example, a future RCT could identify ways to match individuals to the appropriate treatments so that youths who could benefit from brief interventions can do so, while other youths can receive appropriate in-depth treatments such as CBT.

Mental Health Intervention: AFFIRM

Shelley Craig (University of Toronto) described her work on AFFIRM, an affirmative cognitive behavioral intervention to improve mental health of SGM youth. AFFIRM is an eight-session CBT intervention that focuses on promoting positive change and healthy coping through a safe, affirming, and collaborative group therapy experience. It was created, Craig said, to counter "conversion therapy" and its associated harmful narratives. The goals of AFFIRM are to help youths to decrease unhelpful thoughts that may have roots in stigma and homo/bi/transphobia, to feel better about themselves and their lives, and to cope in ways that affirm their identities and support healthy behaviors and actions. AFFIRM was developed using community-member and youth input, with the intention of ensuring an inclusive and affirming stance; recognizing SGM-specific sources of stress (e.g., heterosexism); focusing on the unique experiences of navigating SGM identities during adolescence and young adulthood; and delivering CBT content within an affirming framework that attends to the intersectionality of identity-based experiences (Austin and Craig, 2015; Craig et al., 2013). The program was systematically developed using the adapt-and-evaluate framework, and it is grounded in the realities of mental health service delivery, said Craig. For example, AFFIRM can be delivered in natural settings such as schools, and it can be easily integrated into existing programs. Craig noted that this is important, as it avoids placing an added burden on community-based organizations that are often doing a great deal of work with limited resources.

The implementation of AFFIRM began in 2014 with an open pilot feasibility study in an LGBTQ center in Toronto. Since 2017, AFFIRM has been delivered to 461 participants in 16 sites and online, as part of a clinical trial. Over half of the participants had an immigrant or newcomer parent, 35 percent had moderate to severe depression, and 31 percent had previously attempted suicide. Young people participating in AFFIRM identified as a range of gender identities and sexual orientations, including queer, pansexual, asexual, nonbinary, and two-spirit. Results have shown significant impacts in several areas, including reduction in depression, increases in coping and support, increase in hope, and increases in healthy stress and resource appraisal (Craig et al., 2021). Craig noted that hope is a particularly critical outcome, particularly in terms of increasing "pathway" and "agency." Pathway reflects an individual's ability to see a future in which they are successful, happy, and authentic, while agency reflects their self-efficacy in terms of following that path. Participants reported high rates of satisfaction with the program, indicated that they could apply what they learned, and said that they would recommend AFFIRM to others (Craig et al., 2021). One participant said, "This program has had a profound impact on the way that I think and has given me hope that I thought I'd never find."

Craig also shared information about a new intervention that has grown out of AFFIRM, called AFFIRM Caregiver. As others have discussed, said Craig, caregivers and families are essential to the mental health of queer youth. AFFIRM Caregiver is a seven-session intervention that helps caregivers move away from rejecting behaviors, including behaviors that they think are affirming but are not. The program has been implemented in three states with 103 foster parents; researchers found significant improvement in caregiver attitudes, behaviors, and confidence in implementing the skills they learned (Austin et al., 2021). One foster father stated, "I am not the same man that I was." He described a transformation of some of his core beliefs and shared that the intervention impacted his life beyond the skills he learned about caring for LGBTQ youth.

Craig concluded by explaining that she and her colleagues are collecting and analyzing more data on both programs, looking at longer-term outcomes, and launching AFFIRM in new sites.

Mental Health Interventions: The Trevor Project

LGBTQ youth face increased risk of mental health challenges, yet they often face many barriers to accessing mental health services, said Myeshia Price (The Trevor Project). A recent survey (The Trevor Project, 2021b) found that, over the course of a year, nearly half of surveyed LGBTQ youth wanted counseling from a mental health professional but did not receive it. This problem is even more severe for LGBTQ youth of color, with over half the survey respondents in each racial/ethnic group being unable to access desired care, said Price. The most common barrier that youths report is inability to pay for care. Other common barriers include previous negative experiences with care, not wanting to get a parent's permission, and fear of being outed (Green et al., 2020). LGBTQ youth also reported cultural barriers to care and concerns about whether providers are competent to discuss LGBTQ issues. These data, said Price, indicate that there is incredible need for access to LGBTQ-centered mental health services. When preventive mental healthcare is not available, she said, LGBTQ youth often end up in crisis. The Trevor Project was created because there was no crisis service specific to LGBTQ youth, despite their higher rates of suicide, said Price.

The Trevor Project takes a comprehensive approach to suicide prevention and crisis intervention, said Price. The Trevor Project recognizes the role that factors ranging from the macro- to the individual level can have on mental health, said Price. At the macro level, The Trevor Project advocates for LGBTQ-inclusive policies through legislation and litigation. At the exosystem or community level, The Trevor Project's education department provides information and training on how to best support LGBTQ youth and help prevent suicide, and The Trevor Project research department evaluates and disseminates evidence-based approaches for reducing suicide risk for LGBTQ youth. At the micro-, or individual, level, The Trevor Project provides a safe social-networking community for LGBTQ youth, their friends, and their allies. Price noted that this online platform was even more critical during the pandemic because it allowed youths to find affirming connections even when physically isolated. Finally, The Trevor Project offers direct suicide and crisis-intervention services for LGBTQ youth by phone, text, or chat. The Trevor Project's crisis intervention services are critical for LGBTQ youth, said Price, because these youths strongly prefer an LGBTQ-specific approach. A national survey found that 80 percent of LGBTQ youth said that if they needed to contact a crisis line, it was important that the crisis line include a focus on LGBTQ youth (The Trevor Project, 2021a). Further, said Price, 74 percent of youths who have used The Trevor Project crisis services said they would not contact, or were unsure if they would have contacted, another service if The Trevor Project did not exist. Last year, The Trevor Project directly served over 200,000 LGBTQ youths who reached out for support. During their interactions with The Trevor Project, over 90 percent of youths with suicide risk were successfully de-escalated and sustained at the 1-month follow-up contact, Price said.

The Trevor Project is essential for youths in crisis, said Price, but there is also a need to reach young people before they enter crisis. Changes to the mental healthcare system are necessary to meet the needs of the most vulnerable, including LGBTQ youth, Price said. Many LGBTQ youth have challenges finding accessible, affirming care. The COVID-19 pandemic, said Price, provided many technological adaptations that can now be used to address these challenges. For example, mental healthcare can be provided by telephone or videoconferencing; permitting cross-state licensures may also be beneficial for improving access. Platforms that allow asynchronous provision of mental healthcare can make care more accessible, more flexible, and less expensive, and can give youths the potential for privacy if their parents are not supportive.

Concluding her remarks, Price suggested that work to address the mental health needs of LGBTQ youth should apply an intentional, intersectional perspective. LGBTQ youth with multiple identities often face additional stressors such as bias, racism, anti-immigration attitudes, fear of deportation, and stigma, both within and outside the LGBTQ community; these stressors further compound the everyday stresses of being LGBTQ. For example, she said, Black LGBTQ youth have similar rates of mental health issues as non-Black LGBTQ youth, but they tend to have less access to care, more risk factors, and are often targeted for multiple identities. Price said that it is critical that intersectionality and unique factors are specifically addressed as these youths try to navigate the larger society.

Physical Health Intervention: HIV Prevention

There were over 37,000 new diagnoses of HIV in the U.S. in 2018, said Renata Sanders (Johns Hopkins School of Medicine). Two out of ten diagnoses were among youths ages 13–24, and more than 90 percent were among men, particularly Black men who have sex with men (MSM). There are multiple barriers that young people face in accessing HIV testing, prevention, and treatment, she said. Sanders discussed several multilevel strategies to address these barriers that are based in a socioecological framework. This framework recognizes the ability of individuals to make decisions but also acknowledges that individuals exist within interpersonal relationships, within institutions, and within a culture with laws and policies (Figure 5-1).

Sanders described how interventions work at each level, using HIV and PrEP (pre-exposure prophylaxis that people can take to prevent getting HIV) as an example. At the individual level, a person's knowledge, perceived risk, and enabling factors impact whether they seek care, said Sanders. One intervention on this level is community messaging, using sex-positive messages and bright, visually appealing designs to encourage youths to seek out services (Arrington-Sanders et al., 2016). Echoing other presenters, Sanders noted that it can be valuable to "meet youth where they are"; this is often in virtual spaces, she said. At the interpersonal level, youth are impacted

INTERVENTIONS IN MENTAL, EMOTIONAL, AND PHYSICAL HEALTH

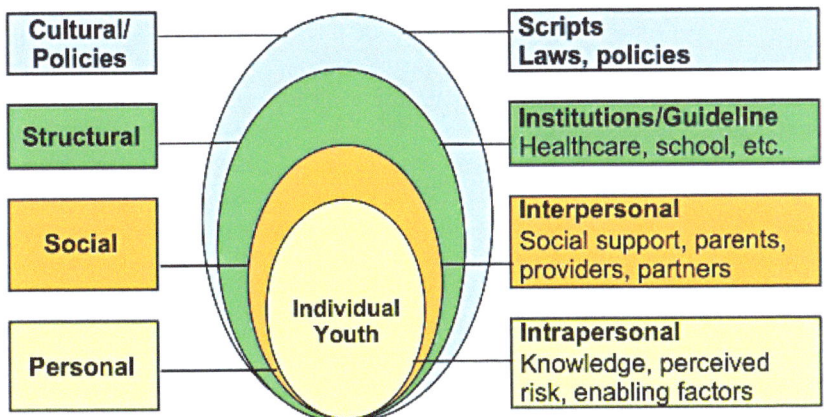

FIGURE 5-1 Socioecological approach to interventions.
SOURCE: Sanders presentation (2021); based on Marcell et al. (2017) and Bronfenbrenner (1977).

by and in relationships with peers, parents, providers, partners, and others. One intervention that works on this level is Providing Unique Support for Health (PUSH), which is a coach-based intervention to engage Black and Latinx MSM and transgender women in HIV treatment and PrEP use. The program is focused on life skills and goal setting; participants reported that health coaches helped them to identify and reach goals, as well as to feel accepted. Parents are also an important interpersonal influence on youths, said Sanders. One promising intervention seeks to help parents and youths talk about sexuality, with a focus on PrEP, through videos and in-person counseling. Sanders noted that these types of interventions can be used not just with parents, but also with other trusted adult figures in a youth's life.

Sanders explained that, at the structural level, HIV and PrEP interventions may include strategies to ensure access to safe housing and employment. A quarter of PUSH participants reported engaging in transactional sex due to housing and job instability; these structural-level interventions are critical for reducing HIV, said Sanders. At the policy level, comprehensive sexual and reproductive health education is essential for reducing HIV infection, said Sanders, yet sexual education varies by state, and eight states restrict teachers from providing LGBTQ-focused education (Raifman et al., 2018).

In his day-one presentation, Bauermeister mirrored Sanders' assessment that interventions on multiple levels are necessary to address HIV in the LGBTQ community. There are a number of HIV interventions, said Bauermeister, some of which are biomedically oriented (e.g., HIV testing) and some of which are more socially oriented (e.g., behavior change strategies). The Prevention Research Synthesis has a searchable compendium[1] of best practices or interventions that have been used by key populations. While there are many interventions for youths, said Bauermeister, many of the evidence-based strategies are "quite old." Bauermeister suggested that there has been a slowing of new evidence that could promote new strategies for LGBTQ youth and that could help re-imagine how older evidence-based practices could be adapted for today's youth. When considering interventions, it is critical that "we're not doing a plug-and-play," said Bauermeister. There is no one-size-fits-all intervention; implementation science can be used to customize, adapt, and scale programs. He noted that technology is an important tool for reaching young people, particularly for SGM youth who may be unable to access information or connection in other ways.

REFLECTIONS

Following the panel presentations, planning committee member Errol Fields (Johns Hopkins School of Medicine) led speakers and participants in a reflective discussion. Workshop audience members were invited to submit questions for panelists via the virtual livestream. Fields opened by noting that the inequities faced by LGBTQ youth, particularly those of color, are the result of intersecting social disadvantages, marginalizations, and oppressions. He asked panelists to comment on whether and how the interventions they described contribute to dismantling those oppressions. Sanders agreed with Field's assessment and said that there is a need for multilevel, comprehensive interventions to address the intersecting identities, disparities, and marginalizations of many LGBTQ youth. Youth have many needs—affirming care providers, comprehensive health education, safe schools—which need to be approached in a culturally congruent way that incorporates intersecting identities and lived experiences. Price added that a multilevel approach is critical to address the multiple factors that impact youth well-being; for example, youths experiencing homelessness are unlikely to be able to adequately treat their anxiety or depression in the absence of stable housing. Price highlighted cost as a primary barrier to mental healthcare access and emphasized that impactful work for youth mental health is already being done in communities of color and could be adapted to become more LGBTQ-affirming. Craig agreed and said that, when implementing individual-level interventions, staff should also be trained to help participants with wraparound services, such as finding housing. She added that implementing interventions within organizations

---

[1] See https://www.cdc.gov/hiv/research/interventionresearch/compendium/index.html.

can help shift the organizational culture and help dismantle oppressions and disadvantages. For example, integrating a caregiver intervention within the foster system can help dismantle transphobia and homophobia, and can "challenge the system in interesting ways." Sanders added that utilizing a peer navigator approach is one way to address multilevel needs while supporting youth. For example, a young person paired with a similar but older peer navigator can get support with navigating internalized homophobia, addressing structural issues such as housing, and seeking physical and mental healthcare. Most importantly, she said, peers can simply "sit with them in that space" and listen to their concerns and worries. She noted that person-to-person engagement is particularly important when interventions are being conducted remotely (e.g., via Zoom).

In concluding her remarks, Price said that improving the mental and physical health of LGBTQ youth cannot be accomplished without addressing the lack of access to affordable physical and mental healthcare. Disparities in access to care "trickle down" to disparities in outcomes for LGBTQ youth of color, said Price. She emphasized that there are many existing interventions—particularly in communities of color—that can be adapted to be inclusive and affirming for LGBTQ populations.

A workshop participant asked speakers to share insights on engaging youth digitally during the COVID-19 pandemic while avoiding "Zoom fatigue." Craig summarized some of AFFIRM's techniques for engaging virtually, including taking frequent breaks during virtual sessions (sometimes involving a walk outdoors), integrating icebreakers and games, and working with co-facilitators so that one facilitator can be active in chat. She also noted that having young people involved in designing digital programming has been essential to engagement. Craig shared that there have been more youths interested in AFFIRM online than offline, and that the virtual format has allowed AFFIRM to provide services to young people who previously experienced barriers to access.

Fields closed the session by asking Price to speak about research on differences in suicide rates among Black youth. Price explained that in her work, she sees the fastest increases in youth suicide rates among Black youth. She also noted that, even when Black and White LGBTQ youth have similar rates of suicide attempts and depression/anxiety, Black LGBTQ youth have less access to care and experience more risk factors. She suggested that this is a vital area for further research.

6

Promising Interventions in Education

On the third day of the workshop, panelists and workshop participants discussed how schools and the educational system can impact the health and well-being of LGBTQ youth, and they identified promising interventions to improve the school environment and to improve health and academic outcomes for LGBTQ youth.

LANDSCAPE: OUTCOMES, INEQUALITIES, AND KNOWN INTERVENTIONS

In schools, LGBTQ youth experience higher levels of bullying, harassment, and victimization from both peers and educators, said Stacey Horn (University of Minnesota). There are disparities in access to affirming and supportive resources, such as inclusive curricula, comprehensive sexual education, use of preferred names and pronouns, and access to bathrooms that match gender identity. LGBTQ youth also experience high levels of exclusionary and punitive discipline, which particularly affects youth of color, and transgender and nonbinary youth. Emerging research, said Horn, documents a link between being bullied and being punished; more research is needed in this area.

Paul Poteat (Boston College) elaborated on issues of harassment and bullying, belonging and inclusion, and discipline. In the past two decades, there have been some tempered improvements in the extent to which LGBTQ youth report harassment, bullying, and discrimination at school, said Poteat (Poteat et al., 2020; Goodenow et al., 2016; Birkett et al., 2015). However, he cautioned, it is not clear that there is a linear trend toward improvement;

he noted that sociopolitical events can lead to significant spikes in victimization of LGBTQ youth (Southern Poverty Law Center, 2019; Gower et al., 2018). For example, the current wave of anti-trans legislation in multiple states can impact the school environment. He also cautioned that these data tend to reflect LGBTQ youth as a monolithic group; there is an absence of research examining the school experience for trans and nonbinary youth and LGBTQ youth of color. Youth of color experience multiple oppressions at the same time, he said, and discrimination can be experienced intersectionally (Kosciw et al., 2020; Hatchel and Marx, 2018). Poteat emphasized the importance of recognizing these unique challenges while also recognizing that LGBTQ youth of color "hold exceptional strengths and resilience and have unique sources of social support." Another area in which consistent disparities exist between LGBTQ youth and their peers is in their reports of school safety, belonging, and inclusion. For example, inclusivity can be evaluated by the heteronormativity and cisnormativity of curricula, whether LGBTQ topics are systematically excluded from curricula, and the visibility (or lack thereof) of LGBTQ people in school spaces (Kuhlemeier et al., 2021; Kosciw et al., 2020; Snapp et al., 2015). Disparities in school safety, belonging, and inclusion are wider for trans youth and LGBTQ youth of color, said Poteat (Coulter et al., 2021; Kosciw et al., 2009; Russell and McGuire, 2008). Finally, LGBTQ youth are disproportionately disciplined and punished at school, and there are heightened disparities at the intersections of sexual orientation, gender, and race. LGBTQ youth are more likely to be punished, and to be punished more severely, for the same infractions as their heterosexual and cisgender peers; punishments may include office referrals, suspensions, and expulsions (Horn and Schriber, 2020; Mittleman, 2018; Poteat et al., 2016; Chmielewski et al., 2016; Snapp et al., 2015; Himmelstein and Brückner, 2011).

The health and academic consequences of these disparities are clear, said Horne. She argued that "hostile and toxic" school environments lead to negative outcomes, including compromised mental health, negative coping mechanisms, risk-taking, and poor education outcomes such as lack of engagement. Poteat elaborated on the evidence regarding academic consequences for LGBTQ youth (Day et al., 2018; Sansone, 2019; Kosciw et al., 2013; Poteat et al., 2011; Pearson et al., 2007). LGBTQ youth have higher absenteeism than their peers, said Poteat, with levels further elevated for transgender and nonbinary youth. Often, this is because LGBTQ youth feel unsafe at school, and being absent is one of the few strategies available to avoid victimization and discrimination, said Poteat. There is also evidence suggesting that LGBTQ youth enroll in fewer advanced math and science courses and receive lower grades overall. Despite this, he said, the standardized test scores of LGBTQ students are not necessarily lower than those of their peers. LGBTQ youth are more likely to leave school at least once before attaining a high school degree or equivalent, and they are less likely to apply to college, attend college, or complete college (Sansone, 2019; Pearson and Wilkinson, 2017; Aragon et al., 2014). There are limited data on long-term outcomes, said Poteat, but there is evidence of workplace discrimination and income inequities for LGBTQ individuals (Cech and Rothwell, 2020; Sears and Mallory, 2011; Carpenter, 2007).

While the disparities are wide and persistent, said Poteat, there is a robust body of research on interventions that can ameliorate some of these disparities (Ioverno et al., 2021; Poteat et al., 2020; Kull et al., 2016; Marx and Kettrey, 2016; Hatzenbuehler et al., 2015b; Snapp et al., 2015; Russell et al., 2010). Poteat highlighted four main categories of interventions:

1. Inclusive and enumerated policies[1] that cover issues such as discrimination, bullying, harassment, and inclusive access for transgender and nonbinary youth;
2. Ongoing educator professional development to teach about sexual orientation and gender identity, the biases that LGBTQ youth face and the consequences of these biases, and how to intervene and improve school climate;
3. Student-based support groups such as GSAs; and
4. Inclusive curricula and school resources.

These interventions have been shown to reduce disparities and improve the health and well-being of LGBTQ students, said Horn. LGBTQ-inclusive and enumerated policies are associated with a more positive school climate, decreased bullying and harassment, and increased student well-being and success. LGBTQ-supportive teachers are associated with an increased perception of safety and belonging, better attendance, and higher academic performance. Educator professional development around LGBTQ issues is associated with decreased bullying and harassment, more positive school climate, and increased student well-being and success. Participating in an LGBTQ school support group or GSA is associated with an increased sense of school safety and belonging, higher academic performance, increased civic involvement and participation, and more positive mental and physical health. Even for students who do not participate in the school GSA or club, the mere presence of the club is related to an increased sense of school safety, said Horn. LGBTQ-inclusive curricula lead to decreased bullying and harassment, a more positive school climate, increased sense of school safety, and higher levels of school attendance. Other resources inclusive of LGBTQ identities (e.g., sex education, library information) have led to

---

[1] Sexual orientation and gender identity are included as categories, and the policies enumerate protections for these specific categories.

more positive school climate, perceptions that adults are supportive and fair, and increased student well-being. In short, said Horn, reducing bullying, harassment, and discrimination, and increasing access and support lead to a more positive school climate and an increased sense of safety and belonging. In turn, these outcomes are related to increased overall well-being, more positive mental and physical health, and higher levels of school engagement and academic success. While Horn noted that this may not seem like a complex set of interventions, implementation can be complicated. This is in part because schools are state governed and there are few federal policies addressing issues of school safety and belonging. As a result, school contexts can vary significantly across states and school districts.

To complement these formal interventions, said Poteat, there is a need to recognize the value of practices and relationships within the school environment; a respectful and affirming school climate is key to ensuring LGBTQ youth safety (Poteat et al., 2021; Kosciw et al., 2020; Colvin et al., 2019; Day et al., 2019; Gower et al., 2018). Encouragingly, said Poteat, research indicates that a large majority of LGBTQ youth can name more than one adult at school who is supportive and willing to help. In addition to teachers and staff, LGBTQ youth look to their peers for mutual support.

Horn identified several knowledge gaps that would benefit from more research. Compared to lesbian and gay youth, less is known about types of interventions that can improve the well-being of trans and nonbinary youth, bisexual youth, and LGBTQ youth of color. Most available evidence is on interventions to reduce negative outcomes; less is known about interventions that enhance positive youth development. More research on the ways school-level supports relate to other system contexts (e.g., juvenile justice), and the impact of macro-level strategies, such as state policies on training, would also be valuable. Poteat noted that there is a gap in research on the ways policies and practices work in combination to shape the school experiences of LGBTQ youth. He concurred with Horn about the need to identify ways to adapt or tailor interventions for specific groups of LGBTQ youth, such as youth of color or trans and nonbinary youth. Finally, said Poteat, targeted research is needed on academic outcomes for LGBTQ youth, including learning processes, academic performance, and career preparation and advancement.

In closing, Horn identified several promising approaches for implementing interventions and furthering the evidence base, including whole-school and whole-district strategies, multisector collaborations, and practice-to-research-to-practice partnerships. These approaches require courageous leadership at all levels, she said.

PROMISING INTERVENTIONS

School-Based Intervention:
Broward County Public Schools' LGBTQ+ Coordinator

Kezia Gilyard is the LGBTQ coordinator for Broward County Public Schools. Gilyard noted that Broward County was the first district in the state of Florida, and one of the very first in the nation, to dedicate a full-time, paid position to supporting LGBTQ students. Gilyard shared their experiences in this role. They highlighted how important it is for those who are working to support LGBTQ students to become knowledgeable about their privilege and the people that they serve. Gilyard noted that, while many advocates aim to dissect and dismantle systems of oppression, it is also valuable to be aware of one's own privileges and how they "show up when we are trying to serve others." Gilyard also highlighted the value of offering a full-time paid position for staff supporting and advocating for LGBTQ students. Gilyard was previously a classroom teacher and was doing work to support LGBTQ youth as a volunteer before their current full-time role was created.

Gilyard emphasized the importance of training teachers, staff, and administrators for improving the health and well-being of LGBTQ students. Professional development can be tiered, they said, with a small group of professionals receiving the most advanced training, a larger group receiving a medium amount of training, and everyone receiving basic training. Staff benefit from courses that are available at various times of the day and the week, and incentives can encourage participation (e.g., direct payments, certificates, awards, additional resources). Gilyard emphasized that all staff benefit from training, including school resource officers and other security staff; and noted that a variety of roles benefit from training that is specific to their responsibilities in schools

Supporting trans students is an important part of advocating for LGBTQ students, said Gilyard. As LGBTQ coordinator, Gilyard develops a trans accommodation plan for any student who needs one. This plan includes details about the bathrooms and locker rooms that the student will use and ensures that staff understand the student's rights and privileges. Students are given the option to involve their parents; "we never out students," Gilyard said. Gilyard holds a meeting with the student, counselors, social workers, parents, and other involved parties, and they discuss a breadth of topics, from mental health to survival sex work to involvement in sports. The record of the meeting usually "only sits with one person" and privacy, confidentiality, and safety are paramount concerns in the meeting process and in records management.

Gilyard encouraged those who work with youth to "advertise that you are an ally." They noted that many young people they work with assume that all adults are homophobic or transphobic, and said that allies who want to create safe spaces need to "queer up" their spaces. For example, Broward County offers badges, posters, stickers, and other resources for people to show their allyship. Another of Gilyard's responsibilities is coordinating the youth-led district GSA summit. Gilyard stressed that they do not plan the summit and highlighted the importance of youths planning events for youths because youths know best what other youths need to get out of the events and programs.

Gilyard also emphasized the importance of engaging with leadership, both in schools and in the community. As a school district employee, Gilyard said, red tape prevents them from doing certain things. Likewise, the work of community organizations is restricted because these organizers do not operate in schools. Gilyard holds meetings that bring together the school superintendent, parents, students, principals, teachers, counselors, and community organizations to discuss how to collaborate to best support students and fill gaps in support between school, family, and community. For example, the school district partners with an organization that matches LGBTQ mentors with LGBTQ mentees, similar to the Big Brother/Big Sister program. Another collaboration includes the Safe to Be Me Coalition, which engages students, educators, families, community partners, healthcare professionals, faith leaders, and other professionals who work directly with children and want to ensure that LGBTQ students thrive. Gilyard noted that the LGBTQ coordinator position has no budget. As a result, Gilyard has to be creative with grants and find innovative ways to pay for events and resources, including through the previously mentioned community collaborations. Gilyard said it is very important that events are free and accessible to all, with an emphasis on ensuring that the most vulnerable members of the population are centered. Finally, Gilyard pointed workshop participants to the Broward County LGBTQ Critical Support Guide,[2] a free resource to help schools improve the health and well-being of LGBTQ students.

School-Based Intervention: Comprehensive Sex Education

Alison Macklin (Sexuality Information and Education Council of the United States) focused her presentation on comprehensive sex education (CSE), a programmatic K–12 framework that focuses on developmentally and age-appropriate sex education and information. Macklin explained that CSE involves more than talking about reproduction and disease prevention, it also covers soft skills such as communication and decision making, and engages students with information "outside of the typical heterosexual

---

[2] See https://www.browardschools.com/lgbtq.

lens," including information on gender identity and sexual orientation. As a K–12 framework, CSE is implemented through a scaffolding process. For example, younger children learn basic information about consent by talking about hugging; this information can be built on as a student grows up.

To support the implementation of CSE, the Sexuality Information and Education Council of the United States (SIECUS) developed and published the National Sex Education Standards in conjunction with sexual health experts and child development experts. Like math or literacy standards, these standards can assist schools in designing and delivering sex education at every grade level, said Macklin. In addition to developing the national standards, SIECUS advances CSE through policy, advocacy, education, and communication. Currently, 33 states and the District of Columbia mandate sex education; however, 13 of these states do not require the education to be age appropriate, medically accurate, culturally responsive, or evidence based. Only 9 states require culturally responsive sex education and HIV/sexually transmitted infection (STI) instruction, and only 10 states have policies that include affirming sexual orientation instruction on LGBTQ identities or discussion of sexual health for LGBTQ youth. Macklin also noted that 7 states explicitly require instruction that discriminates against LGBTQ people.

Macklin emphasized that when young people receive sex education, they have better sexual health outcomes, such as fewer unintended pregnancies and STIs. However, said Macklin, CSE encompasses much more than pregnancy and STI reduction. Research demonstrates that youths who engage in a CSE curriculum have better social and emotional well-being. CSE is holistic, inclusive, trauma-informed, and focuses on reproductive justice. Further, Macklin explained, CSE can help create a culture shift on issues including LGBTQ equality, sexual violence prevention, gender equity, reproductive justice, and dismantling white supremacy. CSE shifts the sex education dialogue away from heteronormativity, said Macklin, and acknowledges and affirms sexual orientation and gender identity in a positive way.

Education policy is largely made at the state and local level, noted Macklin. At the federal level, there is opportunity for positive change in terms of promoting existing civil and human rights; in addition, the Real Education and Access for Healthy Youth Act was recently introduced. This law would ensure that all public schools receive CSE based on the national framework, and would provide funds to school districts for implementation, training, and purchasing of curricula. At the state level, there is model legislation called the Healthy Youth Act, which would ensure that comprehensive curricula are taught in schools that offer sex education. As of the date of the workshop, the Healthy Youth Act had been passed in Colorado, California, and Illinois. On the local level, SIECUS works with school boards to assure that policies are inclusive and supportive of all young people, regardless of orientation or identity.

Macklin identified several interventions that would help advance CSE. First, she said, CSE is best supported when community members, parents, and students understand what is being taught in their schools. Second, CSE can be better supported when the sex-education conversation acknowledges that CSE can also create culture change, create safe spaces for students, and help students become more respectful and inclusive. Third, CSE can be advanced when the public participates in policy-related discussions about changes to sexual education, whether the proposed changes are positive or negative. Fourth, CSE can be advanced in an incremental way, said Macklin. For example, last year, language was removed from an Alabama bill that would have criminalized homosexuality, impacting the ability of sex education programs to address sexual orientation and gender identity in their curricula. Finally, Macklin called on advocates to work against the well-funded opponents of CSE. This vocal minority's goal, she said, is to stop comprehensive sex education "because they know how powerful it can be in changing not only school culture and climate but the societal culture."

School-Based Intervention: GSA Clubs

GSA Network works to support GSA youth clubs in California and across the country, said Geoffrey Winder (GSA Network). GSA clubs were previously called Gay Straight Alliance clubs and are now referred to as either Genders and Sexualities Alliance clubs or just GSA clubs; some have creative names such as Rainbow Club or Diversity Club. In California, the majority of the students in GSA clubs are youth of color. However, said Winder, there are limitations on how GSAs support trans and queer youth of color. GSA Network's tagline, said Winder, is "Trans and queer youth uniting for racial and gender justice." This motto acknowledges that outcomes and conditions for LGBTQ youth of color cannot be improved without addressing the systemic issues that face youth of color in general, for example, the school-to-prison pipeline. LGBTQ youth of color are impacted by racism, homophobia, and transphobia, said Winder, and the intersection of these oppressions has unique consequences. Many LGBTQ youth of color are "pushed out" of the traditional education system and end up in alternative education settings or the juvenile justice system. In the California juvenile justice system, about 20 percent of male-identified youths and 40 percent of female-identified youths are LGBTQ.

Research demonstrates that GSA clubs improve the school climate for students, but Winder noted that they do not necessarily improve school climate in the same way for all students. GSAs can either support or further isolate trans and queer youth of color. For example, in schools where the student population is majority youth of color and the GSA reflects this diversity, the GSA may improve outcomes. However, in schools where youth of color are a minority in both the school and the GSA, the GSA may not feel like a welcoming space, he said.

One role of GSAs is to hold schools accountable for implementing inclusive and supportive policies. For example, the California Healthy Youth Act was passed several years ago, but many school districts still do not teach comprehensive and inclusive sex education. GSA clubs can use their positions to encourage their schools to follow the law. Another role for GSAs is addressing health and wellness for students, for example, reducing stigma around seeking mental health support. This has been particularly important during the COVID-19 pandemic, said Winder, as many students have coped with prolonged isolation while potentially living in home environments that are not welcoming or affirming.

Winder identified three policies that increase disparities and endanger LGBTQ youth of color. First, zero tolerance anti-bullying policies can be problematic because the person who bullied and the person being bullied are treated the same. For example, a student of color or LGBTQ student may be disciplined for a conflict that built up over time, or for "the one time that they responded to the bullying." Such policies punish students without addressing the root cause of the bullying, said Winder, and can contribute to the perpetuation of the school-to-prison pipeline. He described a common situation in which a student bullies other students as a way to distance themselves from an LGBTQ identity, before eventually identifying as LGBTQ. Dress codes are another type of policy that can contribute to disproportionate punishment. Some dress codes are gender specific, leading to obvious problems for gender-nonbinary youth, while others are gender neutral but are implemented in a way that disproportionately affects LGBTQ students. Finally, Winder noted that punitive and exclusionary discipline practices can push trans and queer youth of color out of educational environments; these policies are designed to remove students from schools, and he said trans and queer youth of color are often the first to be removed.

REFLECTIONS

Following the panel presentations, planning committee member Jessica Fish (University of Maryland) led speakers and participants in a reflective discussion. Workshop audience members were invited to submit questions for panelists via the virtual livestream. Fish began by asking speakers to talk about their experiences with resistance to the initiatives and interventions presented, and to describe how they overcame that resistance. Gilyard began by stating, "There is resistance to everything that is LGBTQ-related in school." For example, a parent in Gilyard's district complained about gender-neutral restrooms. Gilyard "gave her the respect of listening first," and then explained that the single-stall restrooms were already gender neutral, and the only change was adding a sign to reflect that. Gilyard said that respectful listening worked to overcome the woman's resistance, and she "calmed down." In the realm of sex education, said Macklin, a minority of people are opposed and are quite vocal about it. Their arguments, said Macklin, are difficult to refute because they are based on misinformation and they use fear-based language that appeals to some people (e.g., the language of "parental rights"). While this is a constant battle, most students and parents want comprehensive sex education, Macklin said.

Fish followed up with a question about what type of supports—whether resources or people—are necessary to do this work well. Macklin noted that, in her experience, "parent power" has been the most helpful in supporting LGBTQ youth-affirming programs. Young people often bring attention to things that need to change, and when parents get involved, change tends to happen, particularly at the local level. Those interested in supporting the well-being of LGBTQ youth would benefit from engaging with parent-teacher associations and similar groups to mobilize grassroots support in favor of LGBTQ-affirming policies and practices. Winder said that some of the "easiest wins" happen when the school principal or superintendent is on board with an intervention. In certain cases, rather than mobilizing community support, "we just take the case to the decision maker," Winder explained. Gilyard said that the most important support in their work is a large and diverse group of stakeholders who are on the same page; Gilyard works with superintendents, board members, parents, students, nonprofits, community partners, and others to collaborate for the health and well-being of LGBTQ students.

A workshop participant asked speakers to comment on best practices for working at the elementary school level. Gilyard replied that much of their work is in elementary schools. They explained that when there is a queer or trans student in an elementary school, the school reaches out for help, "usually in a panic." In middle or high school, a gay or trans student is less of a surprise, and the school tends to "let them mind their business unless something is going wrong." Gilyard noted that they have seen significant pushback when parents try to start GSAs in elementary schools. They noted that a local nonprofit hosts support groups for LGBTQ elementary school children, and Gilyard usually encourages parents and children to go there rather than dealing with the school. Gilyard noted this type of situation as a reason to seek out and remain engaged with community partners. Macklin said that elementary school is the perfect place to start the education about bodies, sex, gender, autonomy, consent, and other topics in CSE. Young children "don't have a filter" and are generally not embarrassed when talking about these concepts, she said, so starting early presents an opportunity to normalize topics of sex and sexuality and create meaningful culture change.

7

Closing Reflections

Stephen Russell (University of Texas at Austin) closed the workshop by asking planning committee members to reflect on what they heard over the 3 days of the workshop. He began with his observation that there are significant gaps between the existing scientific evidence and what we know to be true in communities. He noted both "how far we have come and how far we have to go." Because today's young people are one of the first generations of SGM youth to "express themselves in the full richness of themselves," Russell said, we are still building the societal, institutional, policy, and cultural systems and spaces for LGBTQ young people to thrive. Jessica Fish reflected that LGBTQ young people are "truly inspiring" in terms of their resilience and advocacy. Errol Fields agreed that the advocacy of LGBTQ young people is impressive and emphasized the importance of supporting and partnering with LGBTQ youth in efforts to achieve equity. He also highlighted that adults are responsible for driving the systemic changes required to achieve equity. Fields said that we "shouldn't be relying on youths to fix the problems that were here before they got here." Nat Duran emphasized the need to identify and leverage "pressure points" that can shift resources toward community-based organizations that are already making change happen.

Jama Shelton said that, as a person who grew up in rural Mississippi and didn't "know another gay person until I was 19," this workshop was impactful. "I am [hearing] the ancestors who have fought for a day like this," added Amorie Robinson. She said that the workshop was a historic opportunity to share ideas, learn about the work being done, connect, and inspire. In closing, Robinson called for systemic change, more partnerships between research, practice, and community, and an earnest focus on LGBTQ youth of color, nonbinary youth, and gender-nonconforming youth.

References

Abreu, R., Sostre, J., Gonzalez, K., Lockett, G., and Matsuno, E. 2021. "I am afraid for those kids who might find death preferable": Parental figures' reactions and coping strategies to bans on gender affirming care for transgender and gender diverse youth. *Psychology of Sexual Orientation and Gender Diversity*. doi: 10.1037/sgd0000495.

Aragon, S.R., Poteat, V.P., Espelage, D.L., and Koenig, B.W. 2014. The influence of peer victimization on educational outcomes for LGBTQ and non-LGBTQ high school students. *Journal of LGBT Youth*, 11(1), 1–19. doi: 10.1080/19361653.2014.840761.

Arrington-Sanders, R., Morgan, A., Oidtman, J., Qian, I., Celentano, D., and Beyrer, C. 2016. A medical care missed opportunity: Preexposure prophylaxis and young black men who have sex with men. *The Journal of Adolescent Health*, 59(6), 725–728. doi: https://doi.org/10.1016/j.jadohealth.2016.08.006.

Austin, A., and Craig, S.L. 2015. Transgender affirmative cognitive behavioral therapy: Clinical considerations and applications. *Professional Psychology: Research and Practice*, 46(1), 21–29.

Austin, A., Craig, S.L., Matarese, M., Greeno, E.J., Weeks, A., and Betsinger, S.A. 2021. Preliminary effectiveness of an LGBTQ+ affirmative parenting intervention with foster parents. *Children and Youth Services Review*. doi: https://doi.org/10.1016/j.childyouth.2021.106107.

Balaji, A.B., Bowles, K.E., Le, B.C., Paz-Bailey, G., Oster, A.M., and NHBS Study Group. 2013. High HIV incidence and prevalence and associated factors among young MSM. 2008. *AIDS*, 27(2), 269–278. doi: https://doi.org/10.1097/QAD.0b013e32835ad489.

Bauermeister, J.A., Golinkoff, J.M., Lin, W.Y., Claude, K.F., Horvath, K.J., Dowshen, N., Schlupp, A., Vickroy, W.J., Desir, K., Lopez, A.V., Castillo, M., Tanney, M., Wimbly, T.A., Leung, K., Sullivan, P.S., Santiago, D.L., Hernandez, R., Paul, M.E., Hightow-Weidman, L., Lee, S., and Stephenson, R. 2019. Testing the testers: Are young men who have sex with men receiving adequate HIV testing and counseling services? *Journal of Acquired Immune Deficiency Syndromes*, 82 Suppl 2(2), S133–S141. doi: https://doi.org/10.1097/QAI.0000000000002173.

Berger, C., Poteat, P.V., and Dantas, J. 2017. Should I report? The role of general and sexual orientation-specific bullying policies and teacher behavior on adolescents' reporting of victimization experiences. *Journal of School Violence*, 18(1), 107–120. doi: https://doi.org/10.1080/15388220.2017.1387134.

Birkett, M., Newcomb, M E., and Mustanski, B. 2015. Does it get better? A longitudinal analysis of psychological distress and victimization in lesbian, gay, bisexual, transgender, and questioning youth. *The Journal of Adolescent Health*, 56(3), 280–285. doi: https://doi.org/10.1016/j.jadohealth.2014.10.275.

Bishop, M.D., Fish, J.N., Hammack, P.L., and Russell, S.T. 2020. Sexual identity development milestones in three generations of sexual minority people: A national probability sample. *Developmental Psychology*, Advance online publication. doi: http://dx.doi.org/10.1037/dev0001105.

Bochicchio, L., Reeder, K., Ivanoff, A., Pope, H., and Stefancic, A. 2020. Psychotherapeutic interventions for LGBTQ + youth: A systematic review. *Journal of LGBT Youth*, doi: 10.1080/19361653.2020.1766393.

Bronfenbrenner, U. 1977. Toward an experimental ecology of human development. *American Psychologist*, 32(7), 513–531. doi: https://doi.org/10.1037/0003-066X.32.7.513.

Burns, M.N., Ryan, D.T., Garofalo, R., Newcomb, M.E., and Mustanski, B. 2015. Mental health disorders in young urban sexual minority men. *The Journal of Adolescent Health*, 56(1), 52–58. doi: https://doi.org/10.1016/j.jadohealth.2014.07.018.

Carpenter, C. 2007. Revisiting the earnings penalty for behaviorally gay men: Evidence from NHANES III. *Labour Economics*, 14(1), 25–34.

Cech, E., and Rothwell, W.R. 2020. LGBT workplace inequality in the federal workforce: Intersectional processes, organizational contexts, and turnover considerations. *Industrial and Labor Regulations Review*, (73)1. doi: https://doi.org/10.1177/0019793919843508.

Celentano, D.D., Valleroy, L.A., Sifakis, F., MacKellar, D.A., Hylton, J., Thiede, H., McFarland, W., Shehan, D.A., Stoyanoff, S.R., LaLota, M., Koblin, B.A., Katz, M.H., Torian, L.V., and Young Men's Survey Study Group. 2006. Associations between substance use and sexual risk among very young men who have sex with men. *Sexually Transmitted Diseases*, 33(4), 265–271. doi: https://doi.org/10.1097/01.olq.0000187207.10992.4e.

CDC (Centers for Disease Control and Prevention). 2021. *YRBSS Data and Documentation*. Atlanta, GA: U.S. Department of Health and Human Services. Available: https://www.cdc.gov/healthyyouth/data/yrbs/data.htm.

Chmielewski, J., Belmonte, K., Fine, M., and Stoudt, B. 2016. "Intersectional inquiries with LGBTQ and gender nonconforming youth of color: Participatory research on discipline disparities at the race/sexuality/gender nexus." Inequality in school discipline. Palgrave Macmillan, New York, 2016. 171–188. doi: 10.1057/978-1-137-51257-4_10.

Clark, K.A., Cochran, S.D., Maiolatesi, A.J., and Pachankis, J.E. 2020. Prevalence of bullying among youth classified as LGBTQ who died by suicide as reported in the National Violent Death Reporting System, 2003–2017. *JAMA Pediatrics*, 174(12), 1211–1213. doi:10.1001/jamapediatrics.2020.0940.

Colvin, S., Egan, J.E., and Coulter, R. 2019. School climate and sexual and gender minority adolescent mental health. *Journal of Youth and Adolescence*, 48(10), 1938–1951. doi: https://doi.org/10.1007/s10964-019-01108-w.

Conron, K. 2020. *LGBT Youth Population in the United States*. UCLA School of Law, CA: Williams Institute. Available: https://williamsinstitute.law.ucla.edu/publications/lgbt-youth-pop-us.

Coulter, R.W., Kenst, K.S., Bowen, D.J., and Scout. 2014. Research funded by the National Institutes of Health on the health of lesbian, gay, bisexual, and transgender populations. *American Journal of Public Health*, 104(2), e105–e112. doi: https://doi.org/10.2105/AJPH.2013.301501.

REFERENCES

Coulter R., Sang J., Louth-Marquez W., Henderson E., Espelage, D., Hunter, S., DeLucas, M., Abebe, K., Miller, E., Morrill, B., Hieftje, K., Friedman, M., and Egan, J. 2019. Pilot testing the feasibility of a game intervention aimed at improving help seeking and coping among sexual and gender minority youth: Protocol for a randomized controlled trial. *JMIR Research Protocols*, 8(2), e12164. doi: 10.2196/12164.

Coulter, R.W., Paglisotti, T., Montano, G., Bodnar, K., Bersamin, M., Russell, S.T., Hill, A.V., Mair, C., and Miller, E. 2021. Intersectional differences in protective school assets by sexuality, gender, race/ethnicity, and socioeconomic status. *Journal of School Health*, 91(4), 318–330. doi: 10.1111/josh.13005.

Craig, S.L., Austin, A., and Alessi, E. 2013. Gay affirmative cognitive behavioral therapy for sexual minority youth: A clinical adaptation. *Clinical Social Work Journal*, 41(3), 258–266.

Craig S.L., McInroy L.B., Eaton A.D., Iacono G., Leung V.W., Austin A., and Dobinson, C. 2019. An affirmative coping skills intervention to improve the mental and sexual health of sexual and gender minority youth (Project Youth AFFIRM): Protocol for an implementation study. *JMIR Research Protocols*, 8(6), e13462. doi: 10.2196/13462.

Craig, S.L., Leung, V., Pascoe, R., Pang, N., Iacono, G., Austin, A., and Dillon, F. 2021. AFFIRM online: Utilising an affirmative cognitive-behavioural digital intervention to improve mental health, access, and engagement among LGBTQA+ youth and young adults. *International Journal of Environmental Research and Public Health*, 18(4), 1541. doi: https://doi.org/10.3390/ijerph18041541.

Czeisler, M.É., Lane, R.I., Petrosky, E., Wiley, J.F., Christensen, A.,Njai, R., Weaver, M.D., Robbins, R., Facer-Childs, E.R., Barger, L.K., Czeisler, C.A., Howard, M.E., and Rajaratnam, S.M.W. 2020. Mental health, substance use, and suicidal ideation during the COVID-19 pandemic—United States, June 24–30, 2020. *Morbidity and Mortality Weekly Report*, 69(32), 1049–1057. doi: http://dx.doi.org/10.15585/mmwr.mm6932a1.

Day, J.K., Fish, J.N., Perez-Brumer, A., Hatzenbuehler, M.L., and Russell, S.T. 2017. Transgender youth substance use disparities: Results from a population-based sample. *The Journal of Adolescent Health*, 61(6), 729–735. doi: https://doi.org/10.1016/j.jadohealth.2017.06.024.

Day, J.K., Perez-Brumer, A., and Russell, S.T. 2018. Safe schools? Transgender youth's school experiences and perceptions of school climate. *Journal of Youth and Adolescence*, 47(8), 1731–1742.

Day, J.K., Ioverno, S., and Russell, S.T. 2019. Safe and supportive schools for LGBT youth: Addressing educational inequities through inclusive policies and practices. *Journal of School Psychology*, 74, 29–43.

Diamond, G.M., Diamond, G.S., Levy, S., Closs, C., Ladipo, T., and Siqueland, L. 2012. Attachment-based family therapy for suicidal lesbian, gay, and bisexual adolescents: A treatment development study and open trial with preliminary findings. *Psychotherapy*, 49(1), 62–71. doi: https://doi.org/10.1037/a0026247.

Earnshaw, V.A., Reisner, S.L., Menino, D., Poteat, V.P., Bogart, L.M., Barnes, T.N., and Schuster, M.A. 2018. Stigma-based bullying interventions: A systematic review. *Developmental Review*, 48, 178–200. doi: https://doi.org/10.1016/j.dr.2018.02.001.

Else-Quest, N.M., and Hyde, J.S. 2016a. Intersectionality in quantitative psychological research: II. Methods and techniques. *Psychology of Women Quarterly*, 40(3), 319–336. doi: https://doi.org/10.1177/0361684316647953.

Else-Quest, N.M., and Hyde, J.S. 2016b. Intersectionality in quantitative psychological research: I. Theoretical and epistemological issues. *Psychology of Women Quarterly*, 40(2), 155–170. doi: https://doi.org/10.1177/0361684316629797.

Espelage, D., Rose, C., and Polanin, J. 2015. Social-emotional learning program to reduce bullying, fighting, and victimization among middle school students with disabilities. *Remedial and Special Education*, 36(5). doi: 10.1177/0741932514564564.

Fields, E.L., Bogart, L.M., Smith, K.C., Malebranche, D.J., Ellen, J., and Schuster, M.A. 2015. "I always felt I had to prove my manhood": Homosexuality, masculinity, gender role strain, and HIV risk among young Black men who have sex with men. *American Journal of Public Health*, 105(1), 122–131. doi: https://doi.org/10.2105/AJPH.2013.301866.

Fish, J.N. 2020. Future directions in understanding and addressing mental health among LGBTQ youth. *Journal of Clinical Child and Adolescent Psychology*, 49(6), 943–956. doi: 10.1080/15374416.2020.1815207.

Fish, J.N., Moody, R.L., Grossman, A.H., and Russell, S.T. 2019. LGBTQ youth-serving community-based organizations: Who participates and what difference does it make? *Journal of Youth and Adolescence*, 48(12), 2418–2431. doi: https://doi.org/10.1007/s10964-019-01129-5.

Fish, J.N., Baams, L., and McGuire, J.K. 2020. Sexual and gender minority mental health issues among children and youth. Pp. 229–244 in *Oxford Handbook of Sexual and Gender Minority Mental Health* (E.D. Rothblum, ed.). New York: Oxford University Press.

Fish, J.N., Williams, N.D., McInroy, L.B., Paceley, M.S., Edsall, R.N., Devadas, J., Birnel Henderson, S., and Levine, D.S. 2021. Q Chat Space: Assessing the feasibility and acceptability of an internet-based support program for LGBTQ youth. *Prevention Science*, doi: https://doi.org/10.1007/s11121-021-01291-y.

GLAAD. n.d. *Conversion Therapy*. Available: https://www.glaad.org/conversiontherapy.

GLSEN. 2018. *Laws Prohibiting "Promotion of Homosexuality" in Schools: Impacts and Implications*. Available: https://www.glsen.org/sites/default/files/2019-10/GLSEN-Research-Laws-that-Prohibit-Promotion-of-Homosexuality-Implications.pdf.

Goodenow, C., Szalacha, L., and Westheimer, K. 2006. School support groups, other school factors, and the safety of sexual minority adolescents. *Psychology in the Schools*, 43, 573–589. doi: 10.1002/pits.20173.

Goodenow, C., Watson, R.J., Adjei, J., Homma, Y., and Saewyc, E. 2016. Sexual orientation trends and disparities in school bullying and violence-related experiences, 1999-2013. *Psychology of Sexual Orientation and Gender Diversity*, 3(4), 386–396. doi: https://doi.org/10.1037/sgd0000188.

Goodman, J.A., and Israel, T. 2020. An online intervention to promote predictors of supportive parenting for sexual minority youth. *Journal of Family Psychology*, 34(1), 90–100. doi: https://doi.org/10.1037/fam0000614.

Gower, A.L., Rider, G.N., McMorris, B.J., and Eisenberg, M.E. 2018. Bullying victimization among LGBTQ youth: Current and future directions. *Current Sexual Health Reports*, 10(4), 246–254. doi: https://doi.org/10.1007/s11930-018-0169-y.

Green, A.E., Price-Feeny, M., and Dorison, S. 2020. *Breaking Barriers to Quality Mental Health Care for LGBTQ Youth*. New York: The Trevor Project. Available: https://www.thetrevorproject.org/research-briefs/breaking-barriers-to-quality-mental-health-care-for-lgbtq-youth.

Greytak, E.A., Kosciw, J.G., Villenas, C., and Giga, N.M. 2016. *From Teasing to Torment: School Climate Revisited, A Survey of U.S. Secondary School Students and Teachers*. New York: GLSEN. Available: https://www.glsen.org/research/teasing-torment-school-climate-revisited-survey-us-seconda.

Hall, W. 2017. The effectiveness of policy interventions for school bullying: A systematic review. *Journal of the Society for Social Work and Research*, 8(1), 45–69.

Hatchel, T., and Marx, R. 2018. Understanding intersectionality and resiliency among transgender adolescents: Exploring pathways among peer victimization, school belonging, and drug use. *International Journal of Environmental Research and Public Health*, 15(6), 1289. doi: https://doi.org/10.3390/ijerph15061289.

Hatzenbuehler, M.L. 2009. How does sexual minority stigma "get under the skin"? A psychological mediation framework. *Psychological Bulletin*, 135(5), 707–730. doi: https://doi.org/10.1037/a0016441.

Hatzenbuehler, M.L. 2011. The social environment and suicide attempts in lesbian, gay, and bisexual youth. *Pediatrics*, 127(5), 896–903. doi: https://doi.org/10.1542/peds.2010-3020.

Hatzenbuehler, M.L., Birkett, M., Van Wagenen, A., and Meyer, I.H. 2014. Protective school climates and reduced risk for suicide ideation in sexual minority youths. *American Journal of Public Health*, 104(2), 279–286. doi: https://doi.org/10.2105/AJPH.2013.301508.

Hatzenbuehler, M.L., Jun, H.J., Corliss, H.L., and Bryn Austin, S. 2015a. Structural stigma and sexual orientation disparities in adolescent drug use. *Addictive Behaviors*, 46, 14–18. doi: https://doi.org/10.1016/j.addbeh.2015.02.017.

Hatzenbuehler, M.L., Schwab-Reese, L., Ranapurwala, S.I., Hertz, M.F., and Ramirez, M.R. 2015b. Associations between antibullying policies and bullying in 25 states. *JAMA Pediatrics*, 169(10), e152411. doi: https://doi.org/10.1001/jamapediatrics.2015.2411.

Himmelstein, K.E., and Brückner, H. 2011. Criminal-justice and school sanctions against nonheterosexual youth: A national longitudinal study. *Pediatrics*, 127(1), 49–57. doi: https://doi.org/10.1542/peds.2009-2306.

Hobaica, S., Alman, A., Jackowich, S., and Kwon, P. 2018. Empirically based psychological interventions with sexual minority youth: A systematic review. *Psychology of Sexual Orientation and Gender Diversity*, 5(3), 313–323.

Horn, S., and Schriber, S. 2020. Bullied and punished: Exploring the links between bullying and discipline for sexual and gender minority youth. *Journal of Research on Adolescence*, 30. doi: 10.1111/jora.12556.

Horn, S.S., and Szalacha, L.A. 2009. School differences in heterosexual students' attitudes about homosexuality and prejudice based on sexual orientation. *European Journal of Developmental Science*, 3, 66–81. doi: https://doi.org/10.3233/DEV-2009-3108.

Horne, S.G., McGinley, M., Yel, N., and Maroney, M.R. 2021. The stench of bathroom bills and anti-transgender legislation: Anxiety and depression among transgender, non-binary, and cisgender LGBQ people during a state referendum. *Journal of Counseling Psychology*. doi: 10.1037/cou0000558.

Huebner, D.M., Rullo, J.E., Thoma, B.C., McGarrity, L.A., and Mackenzie, J. 2013. Piloting Lead with Love: A film-based intervention to improve parents' responses to their lesbian, gay, and bisexual children. *The Journal of Primary Prevention*, 34(5), 359–369. doi: https://doi.org/10.1007/s10935-013-0319-y.

Huebner, D.M., Barnett, A.P., Baucom, B.R.W., and Guilamo-Ramos, V. 2021. Randomized controlled trial of HIV communication intervention for parents of gay/bisexual youth. Submitted.

Ioverno, S., Bishop, M.D., and Russell, S.T. 2021. Does a decade of school administrator support for educator training on students' sexual and gender identity make a difference for students' victimization and perceptions of school climate? *Prevention Science*. doi: 10.1007/s11121-021-01276-x.

Irvine, A., and Canfield, A. 2016. The overrepresentation of lesbian, gay, bisexual, questioning, gender nonconforming and transgender youth within the child welfare to juvenile justice crossover population. *American University Journal of Gender, Social Policy & the Law*, 24(2). doi: http://digitalcommons.wcl.american.edu/jgspl/vol24/iss2/2.

Jackson, S.D., Mohr, J.J., and Kindahl, A.M. 2021. Intersectional experiences: A mixed methods experience sampling approach to studying an elusive phenomenon. *Journal of Counseling Psychology*, 68(3), 299–315. doi: https://doi.org/10.1037/cou0000537.

Johns, M.M., Lowry, R., Haderxhanaj, L.T., Rasberry, C.N., Robin, L., Scales, L., Stone, D., and Suarez, N.A. 2020. Trends in violence victimization and suicide risk by sexual identity among high school students—youth risk behavior survey, United States, 2015–2019. *Morbidity and Mortality Weekly Report*, 69(Suppl-1), 19–27. doi: http://dx.doi.org/10.15585/mmwr.su6901a3.

Jones, J. 2021. LGBT Identification Rises to 5.6% in Latest U.S. Estimate. *Gallup*, February 24. Available: https://news.gallup.com/poll/329708/lgbt-identification-rises-latest-estimate.aspx.

Keefe, J.R., Rodrigues-Seijas, C., Hatzenbuehler, M.L., and Pachankis, J.E. 2021. LGBTQ-affirmative cognitive-behavioral therapy is especially effective among racial/ethnic minority gay and bisexual men. [Unpublished manuscript]. School of Public Health, Yale University.

Kosciw, J.G., Greytak, E.A., and Diaz, E.M. 2009. Who, what, where, when, and why: Demographic and ecological factors contributing to hostile school climate for lesbian, gay, bisexual, and transgender youth. *Journal of Youth and Adolescence*, 38(7), 976–988. doi: https://doi.org/10.1007/s10964-009-9412-1.

Kosciw, J.G., Palmer, N.A., Kull, R.A., and Greytak, E.A. 2013. The effect of negative school climate on academic outcomes for LGBT youth and the role of in-school supports. *Journal of School Violence*, 12(1), 45–63. doi: 10.1080/15388220.2012.732546.

Kosciw, J.G., Greytak, E., Zongrone, A., Clark, C., and Truong, N. 2018. *The 2017 National School Climate Survey: The Experiences of Lesbian, Gay, Bisexual, Transgender, and Queer Youth in Our Nation's Schools*. New York: GLSEN. Available: https://www.glsen.org/sites/default/files/2019-10/GLSEN-2017-National-School-Climate-Survey-NSCS-Full-Report.pdf.

Kosciw, J.G., Clark, C.M., Truong, N.L., and Zongrone, A.D. 2020. *The 2019 National School Climate Survey: The Experiences of Lesbian, Gay, Bisexual, Transgender, and Queer Youth in Our Nation's Schools*. New York: GLSEN. Available: https://www.glsen.org/research/2019-national-school-climate-survey.

Kuhlemeier, A., Goodkind, J., and Willging, C. 2021. Production and maintenance of the institutional in/visibility of sexual and gender minority students in schools. *American Journal of Orthopsychiatry*. 91, 558–568. doi: 10.1037/ort0000556.

Kull, R., Greytak, E., Kosciw, J., and Villenas, C. 2016. Effectiveness of school district anti-bullying policies in improving LGBT youths' school climate. *Psychology of Sexual Orientation and Gender Diversity*, 3, 407–415. doi: 10.1037/sgd0000196.

la Roi, C., Kretschmer, T., Dijkstra, J. K., Veenstra, R., and Oldehinkel, A.J. 2016. Disparities in depressive symptoms between heterosexual and lesbian, gay, and bisexual youth in a Dutch cohort: The TRAILS study. *Journal of Youth and Adolescence*, 45(3), 440–456. doi: https://doi.org/10.1007/s10964-015-0403-0.

Levesque, B. 2021. Alarming number of Texas trans kids in crises over litany of anti-trans bills. *Los Angeles Blade*, September 25. Available: https://www.losangelesblade.com/2021/09/25/alarming-numbers-of-texas-trans-kids-in-crisis-over-litany-of-anti-trans-bills.

Lewis, J.A., Williams, M.G., Peppers, E.J., and Gadson, C.A. 2017. Applying intersectionality to explore the relations between gendered racism and health among Black women. *Journal of Counseling Psychology*, 64(5), 475–486. doi: https://doi.org/10.1037/cou0000231.

Lipson, S.K., Lattie, E.G., and Eisenberg, D. 2019. Increased rates of mental health service utilization by U.S. college students: 10-year population-level trends (2007-2017). *Psychiatric Services*, 70(1), 60–63. doi: https://doi.org/10.1176/appi.ps.201800332.

REFERENCES

Liu, S.R., and Modir, S. 2020. The outbreak that was always here: Racial trauma in the context of COVID-19 and implications for mental health providers. *Psychological Trauma: Theory, Research, Practice, and Policy*, 12(5), 439–442. doi: https://doi.org/10.1037/tra0000784.

Lucassen, M.F., Hatcher, S., Fleming, T.M., Stasiak, K., Shepherd, M.J., and Merry, S.N. 2015. A qualitative study of sexual minority young people's experiences of computerised therapy for depression. *Australasian Psychiatry*, 23(3), 268–273. doi: https://doi.org/10.1177/1039856215579542.

Magnus, M., Kuo, I., Phillips, G., Shelley, K., Rawls, A., Montanez, L., Peterson, J., West-Ojo, T., Hader, S., and Greenberg, A.E. 2010. Elevated HIV prevalence despite lower rates of sexual risk behaviors among Black men in the District of Columbia who have sex with men. *AIDS Patient Care and STDs*, 24(10), 615–622. doi: https://doi.org/10.1089/apc.2010.0111.

Mallory, A.B., and Russell, S.T. 2021. Intersections of racial discrimination and LGB victimization for mental health: A prospective study of sexual minority youth of color. *Journal of Youth and Adolescence*, 50, 1353–1368. doi: https://doi.org/10.1007/s10964-021-01443-x.

Marcell, A.V., Morgan, A.R., Sanders, R., Lunardi, N., Pilgrim, N.A., Jennings, J.M., Page, K.R., Loosier, P.S., and Dittus, P.J. 2017. The socioecology of sexual and reproductive health care use among young urban minority males. *Journal of Adolescent Health*, 60(4), 402–410.

Marx, R.A., and Kettrey, H.H. 2016. Gay-straight alliances are associated with lower levels of school-based victimization of LGBTQ+ youth: A systematic review and meta-analysis. *Journal of Youth and Adolescence*, 45(7), 1269–1282. doi: https://doi.org/10.1007/s10964-016-0501-7.

Matsuno, E., and Israel, T. 2021. The parent support program: Development and acceptability of an online intervention aimed at increasing supportive behaviors among parents of trans youth. *Journal of GLBT Family Studies*, doi: 10.1080/1550428X.2020.1868369.

Meyer, I.H. 2003. Prejudice, social stress, and mental health in lesbian, gay, and bisexual populations: Conceptual issues and research evidence. *Psychological Bulletin*, 129(5), 674–697. doi: https://doi.org/10.1037/0033-2909.129.5.674.

Meyer, I.H., Luo, F., Wilson, B., and Stone, D.M. 2019. Sexual orientation enumeration in state antibullying statutes in the United States: Associations with bullying, suicidal ideation, and suicide attempts among youth. *LGBT Health*, 6(1), 9–14. doi: https://doi.org/10.1089/lgbt.2018.0194.

Mittleman, J. 2018. Sexual orientation and school discipline: New evidence from a population-based sample. *Educational Researcher*, 47(3), 181–190.

Moore J.T., Ricaldi, J.N., Rose, C.E., Fuld, J., Parise, M., Kang, G.J., Driscoll, A.K., Norris, T., Wilson, N., Rainisch, G., Valverde, E., Beresovsky, V., Agnew Brune, C., Oussayef, N.L., Rose, D.A., Adams, L.E., Awel, S., Villanueva, J., Meaney-Delman, D., Honein, M.A., and the COVID-19 State, Tribal, Local, and Territorial Response Team. 2020. Disparities in incidence of COVID-19 among underrepresented racial/ethnic groups in counties identified as hotspots during June 5–18, 2020—22 States, February–June 2020. *Morbidity and Mortality Weekly Report*, 69(33), 1122–1126. doi: http://dx.doi.org/10.15585/mmwr.mm6933e1.

Murchison, G.R., Agénor, M., Reisner, S.L., and Watson, R.J. 2019. School restroom and locker room restrictions and sexual assault risk among transgender youth. *Pediatrics*, 143(6). doi: 10.1542/peds.2018-22902.

Mustanski, B.S., Newcomb, M.E., Du Bois, S.N., Garcia, S.C., and Grov, C. 2011. HIV in young men who have sex with men: A review of epidemiology, risk and protective factors, and interventions. *Journal of Sex Research*, 48(2–3), 218–253. doi: 10.1080/00224499.2011.558645.

NASEM (National Academies of Sciences, Engineering, and Medicine). 2016. *Preventing Bullying Through Science, Policy, and Practice*. Washington, DC: The National Academies Press. doi: https://doi.org/10.17226/23482.

NASEM. 2019. *The Promise of Adolescence: Realizing Opportunity for All Youth*. Washington, DC: The National Academies Press. doi: https://doi.org/10.17226/25388.

NASEM. 2020. *Understanding the Well-Being of LGBTQI+ Populations*. Washington, DC: The National Academies Press. doi: https://doi.org/10.17226/25877.

Newcomb, M.E., LaSala, M.C., Bouris, A., Mustanski, B., Prado, G., Schrager, S.M., and Huebner, D.M. 2019. The influence of families on LGBTQ youth health: A call to action for innovation in research and intervention development. *LGBT Health*, 6(4), 139–145. doi: https://doi.org/10.1089/lgbt.2018.0157.

Ocasio, M.A., Lozano, A., Lee, T.K., Feaster, D.J., Carrico, A., and Prado, G. 2021. Efficacy of a family-based intervention for HIV prevention with Hispanic adolescents with same gender sexual behaviors. *Prevention Science*, doi: https://doi.org/10.1007/s11121-021-01272-1.

Pachankis, J.E. 2014. Uncovering clinical principles and techniques to address minority stress, mental health, and related health risks among gay and bisexual men. *Clinical Psychology*, 21(4), 313–330. doi: https://doi.org/10.1111/cpsp.12078.

Pachankis, J.E., Hatzenbuehler, M., Rendina, H., Safren, S.A., and Parsons, J.T. 2015. LGB-affirmative cognitive-behavioral therapy for young adult gay and bisexual men: A randomized controlled trial of a transdiagnostic minority stress approach. *Journal of Consulting and Clinical Psychology*, 83(5), 875–889. doi: 10.1037/cpp0000037.

Pachankis, J., Clark, K., Burton, C., Hughto, J., Bränström, R., and Keene, D. 2020a. Sex, status, competition, and exclusion: Intraminority stress from within the gay community and gay and bisexual men's mental health. *Journal of Personality and Social Psychology*, 119. doi: 10.1037/pspp0000282.

Pachankis, J.E., McConocha, E.M., Clark, K.A., Wang, K., Behari, K., Fetzner, B.K., Brisbin, C.D., Scheer, J.R., and Lehavot, K. 2020b. A transdiagnostic minority stress intervention for gender diverse sexual minority women's depression, anxiety, and unhealthy alcohol use: A randomized controlled trial. *Journal of Consulting and Clinical Psychology*, 88(7), 613–630.

Pachankis, J.E., Clark, K.A., Klein, D.N., and Dougherty, L.R. 2021a. Early timing and determinants of the sexual orientation disparity in internalizing psychopathology: A prospective cohort study from ages 3 to 15. *Journal of Youth and Adolescence*, Nov 3, 1–3. doi: 10.1007/s10964-021-01532-x.

Pachankis, J.E., Harkness, A., Behari, K., Clark, K.A., McConocha, E.M., Winston, R., Adeyinka, O., Maciejewski, K., Reynolds, J., Bränström, R., Esserman, D.A., Hatzenbuehler, M.L., and Safren, S.A. 2021b. LGBTQ-affirmative cognitive-behavioral therapy for young gay and bisexual men's mental and sexual health: A three-arm randomized controlled trial. [Unpublished manuscript]. School of Public Health, Yale University.

Pearson, J., Muller, C., and Wilkinson, L. 2007. Adolescent same-sex attraction and academic outcomes: The role of school attachment and engagement. *Social Problems*, 54(4), 523–542. doi: https://doi.org/10.1525/sp.2007.54.4.523.

Pearson, J., and Wilkinson, L. 2017. Same-sex sexuality and educational attainment: The pathway to college. *Journal of Homosexuality*, 64(4), 538–576. doi: 10.1080/00918369.2016.1194114.

Poteat, V.P., Mereish, E.H., DiGiovanni, C.D., and Koenig, B.W. 2011. The effects of general and homophobic victimization on adolescents' psychosocial and educational concerns: The importance of intersecting identities and parent support. *Journal of Counseling Psychology*, 58, 597–609.

Poteat, V.P., Scheer, J.R., and Chong, E.S.K. 2016. Sexual orientation-based disparities in school and juvenile justice discipline: A multiple group comparison of contributing factors. *Journal of Educational Psychology*, 108(2), 229–241. doi: https://doi.org/10.1037/edu0000058.

Poteat, V.P., Rivers, I., and Vecho, O. 2020. Membership experiences in gender-sexuality alliances (GSAs) predict increased hope and attenuate the effects of victimization. *Journal of School Psychology*, 79, 16–30. doi: https://doi.org/10.1016/j.jsp.2020.02.001.

Poteat, V.P., Fish, J.N., and Watson, R.J. 2021. Gender-sexuality alliances as a moderator of the association between victimization, depressive symptoms, and drinking behavior among LGBTQ+ youth. *Drug and Alcohol Dependence*, 229, 109140.

Puckett, J.A., Tornello, S., Mustanski, B., and Newcomb, M.E. 2021. Gender variations, generational effects, and mental health of transgender people in relation to timing and status of gender identity milestones. *Psychology of Sexual Orientation and Gender Diversity*. doi: https://doi.org/10.1037/sgd0000391.

Raifman, J., Beyrer, C., and Arrington-Sanders, R. 2018. HIV education and sexual risk behaviors among young men who have sex with men. *LGBT Health*, 5(2), 131–138. doi: https://doi.org/10.1089/lgbt.2017.0076.

Raver, J.L., and Nishii, L.H. 2010. Once, twice, or three times as harmful? Ethnic harassment, gender harassment, and generalized workplace harassment. *Journal of Applied Psychology*, 95(2), 236–254. doi: https://doi.org/10.1037/a0018377.

Russell, S.T., and McGuire, J.K. 2008. Toward Positive Youth Development: Transforming Schools And Community Programs. Pp. 133–149 in *The School Climate for Lesbian, Gay, Bisexual, And Transgender (LGBT) Students*. (M. Shinn and H. Yoshikawa, eds.) Oxford University Press. Available: https://doi.org/10.1093/acprof:oso/9780195327892.003.0008.

Russell, S., Kosciw, J., Horn, S., and Saewyc, E. 2010. Safe schools policy for LGBTQ students. *Social Policy Report*, 24(4), 1–25.

Ryan, C., Russell, S.T., Huebner, D., Diaz, R., and Sanchez, J. 2010. Family acceptance in adolescence and the health of LGBT young adults. *Journal of Child and Adolescent Psychiatric Nursing*, 23(4), 205–213. doi: https://doi.org/10.1111/j.1744-6171.2010.00246.x.

Ryan, C., Toomey, R.B., Diaz, R.M., and Russell, S.T. 2018. Parent-initiated sexual orientation change efforts with LGBT adolescents: Implications for young adult mental health and adjustment. *Journal of Homosexuality*. doi: 10.1080/00918369.2018.1538407.

Sansone, D. 2019. LGBT students: New evidence on demographics and educational outcomes. *Economics of Education Review*, 73. doi: https://doi.org/10.1016/j.econedurev.2019.101933.

Sarno, E.L., Swann, G., Newcomb, M.E., and Whitton, S.W. 2021. Intersectional minority stress and identity conflict among sexual and gender minority people of color assigned female at birth. *Cultural Diversity & Ethnic Minority Psychology*, 27(3), 408–417. doi: https://doi.org/10.1037/cdp0000412.

Sears, B., and Mallory, C. 2011. *Documented Evidence of Employment Discrimination and Its Effects on LGBT People*. UCLA, CA: The Williams Institute. Available: https://escholarship.org/uc/item/03m1g5sg.

Sharek, D., McCann, E., and Huntley-Moore, S. 2021. The design and development of an online education program for families of trans young people. *Journal of LGBT Youth*, 18(2), 188–210. doi: 10.1080/19361653.2020.1712296.

Snapp, S.D., Burdge, H., Licona, A.C., Moody, R.L., and Russell, S.T. 2015. Students' perspectives on LGBTQ-inclusive curriculum. *Equity & Excellence in Education*, 48(2), 249–265. doi: 10.1080/10665684.2015.1025614.

Snapp, S.D., Hoenig, J.M., Fields, A., and Russell, S.T. 2015. Messy, butch, and queer: LGBTQ youth and the school-to-prison pipeline. *Journal of Adolescent Research*, 30(1), 57–82. doi: https://doi.org/10.1177/0743558414557625.

Southern Poverty Law Center. 2019. *Hate at School*. Mongomery, AL: Southern Poverty Law Center. Available: https://www.splcenter.org/sites/ default/files/tt_2019_hate_at_school_report_final_0.pdf.

The Trevor Project. 2017. Unpublished internal data.

The Trevor Project. 2021a. *LGBTQ Youth Suicide Prevention in Schools*. CA: The Trevor Project. Available: https://www.thetrevorproject.org/research-briefs/lgbtq-youth-suicide-prevention-in-schools/.

The Trevor Project. 2021b. *National Survey on LGBTQ Youth Mental Health 2021*. CA: The Trevor Project. Available: https://www.thetrevorproject.org/survey-2021/.

Thoma, B.C., and Huebner, D.M. 2013. Health consequences of racist and antigay discrimination for multiple minority adolescents. *Cultural Diversity & Ethnic Minority Psychology*, 19(4), 404–413. doi: https://doi.org/10.1037/a0031739.

Toomey, R.B., Huynh, V.W., Jones, S.K., Lee, S., and Revels-Macalinao, M. 2017. Sexual minority youth of color: A content analysis and critical review of the literature. *Journal of Gay & Lesbian Mental Health*, 21(1), 3–31. doi: https://doi.org/10.1080/19359705.2016.1217499.

Turban, J.L., Beckwith, N., Reisner, S.L., and Keuroghlian, A.S. 2020. Association between recalled exposure to gender identity conversion efforts and psychological distress and suicide attempts among transgender adults. *JAMA Psychiatry*, 77(1), 68–76. doi:10.1001/jamapsychiatry.2019.2285.

VanDaalen, R.A., and Santos, C.E. 2017. Racism and sociopolitical engagement among lesbian, gay, and bisexual racial/ethnic minority adults. *The Counseling Psychologist*, 45(3), 414–437. doi: https://doi.org/10.1177/0011000017699529.

Voisin, D., Bird, J.D.P., Shiu, C.-S., and Krieger, C. 2013. "It's crazy being a Black, gay youth." Getting information about HIV prevention: A pilot study. *Journal of Adolescence*, 36(1), 111–119.

Wheeler Black, W., Fedewa, A., and Gonzalez, K. 2012. Effects of "safe school" programs and policies on the social climate for sexual-minority youth: A review of the literature. *Journal of LGBT Youth*, 9, 321–339. doi: 10.1080/19361653.2012.714343.

Appendix A

Workshop Agenda

Reducing Inequalities Between LGBTQ Adolescents and Cisgender, Heterosexual Adolescents: A Workshop
August 25, 26, and 27, 2021

DAY ONE	AUGUST 25, 2021 [12:00–4:00 PM ET] *Note: All times listed in Eastern Time*
12:00–12:10	Welcome and Introduction Stephen T. Russell, *Planning Committee Chair*
12:10–12:45	Panel Presentation: Framing, Key Concepts, Definitions Naomi Goldberg, Movement Advancement Project Allen Mallory, Ohio State University Russell Toomey, University of Arizona
12:45–1:00	Questions, Answers, Reflections *Moderator:* Stephen T. Russell, *Planning Committee Chair*
1:00–1:40	Panel Presentation: Research on Reducing Inequalities, Prevention, and Intervention José Bauermeister, University of Pennsylvania Stacey Horn, University of Minnesota John Pachankis, Yale School of Public Health Bianca Wilson, University of California, Los Angeles School of Law, Williams Institute

1:40–1:55	Questions, Answers, Reflections *Moderator*: David Chae, *Planning Committee Member*
1:55–2:10	BREAK
2:10–2:50	Lived Expertise: LGBTQ Youth of Color Manal Vishnoi, Northbrook Pride Youth Program Malcolm Lin, University of Kansas Zarah Khan
2:50–3:05	Questions, Answers, Reflections *Moderator*: Nat Duran, *Planning Committee Member*
3:05–3:45	Panel Presentation: Outcomes and Inequalities for LGBTQ Youth of Color Karina Gattamorta, University of Miami Lilianna Reyes, Ruth Ellis Center Carlos Santos, University of California, Los Angeles Luskin School of Public Affairs
3:45–4:00	Questions, Answers, Reflections *Moderator*: Amorie Robinson, *Planning Committee Member*
4:00	ADJOURN
DAY TWO	AUGUST 26, 2021 [12:00–3:00 PM ET] *Note: All times listed in Eastern Time*
12:00–12:05	Welcome and Introduction Stephen T. Russell, *Planning Committee Chair*
12:05–12:30	Scholar Perspective: Care and Community J. Garrett-Walker, University of Toronto Sarah Mountz, University at Albany
12:30–1:20	Panel Presentation: Promising Practices in Personal, Carceral, and Care Systems Bernadette Brown, National Council on Crime and Delinquency Ghirlandi Guidetti, ACLU of Illinois Angela Weeks, University of Maryland School of Social Work, National Quality Improvement Center

APPENDIX A 85

1:20–1:40	Questions, Answers, Reflections *Moderator*: Aisha N. Canfield, *Planning Committee Member*
1:40–1:55	BREAK
1:55–2:40	Panel Presentation: Promising Practices for Families and Communities David Huebner, George Washington University Deborah Levine, CenterLink, Q Chat Space Benita Ramsey, Rainbow Pride Youth Alliance
2:40–3:00	Questions, Answers, Reflections *Moderator*: Jama Shelton, *Planning Committee Member*
3:00	ADJOURN
DAY THREE	**AUGUST 27, 2021 [12:00–3:00 PM ET]** *Note: All times listed in Eastern Time*
12:00–12:05	Welcome and Introduction Stephen T. Russell, *Planning Committee Chair*
12:05–12:30	Scholar Perspective: Education and Health Paul Poteat, Boston College Margaret Rosario, The Graduate Center, CUNY
12:30–1:15	Panel Presentation: Promising Practices in Mental, Emotional, and Physical Health Shelley Craig, University of Toronto, Factor-Inwentash Faculty of Social Work Myeshia Price, Trevor Project Renata Sanders, Johns Hopkins School of Medicine
1:15–1:30	Questions, Answers, Reflections *Moderator*: Errol Fields, *Planning Committee Member*
1:30–1:45	BREAK
1:45–2:30	Panel Presentation: Promising Practices in Education Kezia Gilyard, Broward County Schools Alison Macklin, Sexuality Information and Education Council of the United States (SEICUS) Geoffrey Winder, GSA Network

2:30–2:45	Questions, Answers, Reflections *Moderator*: Jessica N. Fish, *Planning Committee Member*
2:45–3:00	Closing Reflections *Moderator*: Stephen T. Russell, *Planning Committee Chair*
3:00	ADJOURN

Appendix B

Biographical Sketches of Planning Committee Members and Workshop Speakers

PLANNING COMMITTEE

Stephen T. Russell is Priscilla Pond Flawn Regents professor in child development, chair of the Department of Human Development and Family Sciences, and Amy Johnson McLaughlin director of the School of Human Ecology at the University of Texas at Austin. He is an expert in adolescent and young adult health, with a focus on sexual orientation and gender identity. In addition to his expertise in the study of sexual orientation and health, Russell is an expert in the role of school policies, programs, and practices in supporting adolescent adjustment, achievement, and health. He earned a PhD in sociology at Duke University (1994), a master's degree in sociology at William and Mary (1989), and a bachelor's degree in sociology at Wake Forest University (1988). He has been involved in community and professional organizations throughout his career, including as Human Relations Commissioner in several cities (Durham, NC; Davis, CA; Tucson, AZ). Russell has served on the governing boards of the Society for Research in Child Development, the Sexuality Information and Education Council of the United States (SIECUS), National Council on Family Relations (elected fellow), and the Society for Research on Adolescence (President, 2012-2014). He has previously served on National Academies of Sciences, Engineering, and Medicine consensus committees for *The Promise of Adolescence* (2019) and *Understanding the Well-being of LGBTQI+ Populations* (2020).

Aisha Canfield-Allen, MPP is a director at Ceres Policy Research. Since earning a Master of Public Policy from Mills College, she has conducted research on the disproportionate detention of LGBQ/GNCT BIPOC youth and their pathways into the justice system. She was an investigator on a study that was the first to establish that 20 percent of youth in the justice system identify as LGBQ/GNCT and that 85 percent of those youth are also of color. From her research, there has been a growing awareness of the need for facility/jurisdiction-level data. Canfield-Allen provides training and technical assistance to juvenile probation departments to improve data collection processes that allow agencies to give youth an opportunity to disclose their sexual orientation, gender identity and expression (SOGIE). With this data, jurisdictions can make holistic, data-driven decisions that support young people at the intersections of their multiple identities—particularly race/ethnicity and SOGIE—within the context of their local communities. In addition to supporting detained youth, she serves as an evaluation partner to community-based organizations that are serving as healing and transformative alternatives to traditional justice system responses for LGBQ/GNCT youth, most of whom are also BIPOC. Through her work, Canfield-Allen seeks to reclaim research and data as accessible advocacy tools for BIPOC youth, their families, communities, and the practitioners working on behalf of their well-being and liberation.

David Chae is associate professor in the Department of Social, Behavioral, and Population Sciences, director of the Society, Health, and Racial Equity (SHARE) Lab, and associate dean for research at Tulane University School of Public Health & Tropical Medicine. His doctoral degree is in social epidemiology (Harvard School of Public Health, 2007); he completed postdoctoral research as a Robert Wood Johnson Health & Society Scholar at the University of California, Berkeley, and University of California, San Francisco (2009), in the fields of population health and psychoneuroimmunology. Chae's research focuses on the social determinants of health inequities and embodiment of racism. He studies racism as a social-environmental toxin that shapes the inequitable population-level distribution of disease. As part of this work, he examines the interplay between context, developmental period, behavior, and biology, and links to disease susceptibility and progression. In 2019 he was elected to the Academy of Behavioral Medicine Research, the honorary senior scientist society for those whose research is at the interface of behavior and medicine. He is associate editor of the journal *Health Education & Behavior*, on the Editorial Board of *Cultural Diversity & Ethnic Minority Psychology*, and serves on several scientific research groups.

Nat Duran is a compassion-led and dedicated educator focused on community building and social justice across various realms of youth work. They obtained both their B.A. in Teaching of English (2007) and M.Ed. in

Youth Development (2011) from the University of Illinois at Chicago and have been a champion for putting youth voice to action throughout their adult professional life. Duran previously worked as a high school English teacher in Chicago's public schools, and as a youth advocate and a case manager for older youth in care preparing for independence before joining the Alliance to oversee youth programming. In 2019, Duran served on Illinois' Affirming and Inclusive Schools Task Force which informed the Illinois State Board of Education's guidance and model policy for Supporting Transgender, Nonbinary, and Gender Nonconforming Students.

Errol Fields is an assistant professor of pediatrics at the Johns Hopkins School of Medicine in the Department of Pediatrics, Division of Adolescent/Young Adult Medicine. He is a physician scientist and a board certified pediatrician and adolescent medicine subspecialist. His clinical work focuses on primary and subspecialty care for adolescents and young adults including gender-affirming care, inclusive sexual and reproductive health care, and treatment and prevention of HIV and other sexually transmitted infections. He is the co-founder and co-director of the Emerge Gender and Sexuality Clinic for Children, Adolescents and Young Adults and co-director of PrEP is for Youth Clinic which provides PrEP and other HIV prevention services to Baltimore area youth at risk for HIV acquisition. His research focuses on using mixed methodologies to understand and reduce racial disparities in HIV among young Black, gay, bisexual and other men who have sex with men as well as the evaluation of community-engaged practices for reducing stigma and medical distrust as key barriers to HIV prevention, treatment and research. Fields is also committed to the provision of evidence-based, culturally competent care of sexual minority and gender diverse youth and is involved in undergraduate, graduate, and continuing medical education in this area.

Jessica N. Fish is assistant professor in the Department of Family Science at the University of Maryland School of Public Health, and deputy director for research and evaluation at the CDC-funded University of Maryland Prevention Research Center. With a Ph.D. in Family and Child Sciences (Florida State University, 2014) and a master's degree in Couple and Family Therapy (Purdue University Calumet, 2010), her research centers LGBTQ+ young people and their families, with a specific focus on identifying school, family, and community factors implicated in the positive development and health of LGBTQ+ populations. Fish has published over 75 peer-reviewed publications in top-ranking journals specific to LGBTQ population health and development. Ultimately, her work aims to identify modifiable factors that contribute to LGBTQ-related health disparities in order to inform developmentally-sensitive policies, programs, and prevention strategies that promote the health of sexual and gender minority people across the life course. Fish's most recent scholarship incorporates a community-engaged approach designed to accelerate translational science and bridge the research-to-practice gap for addressing LGBTQ+ youth mental health and substance use in family and community contexts.

Amorie Robinson is a clinical psychologist in metro Detroit serving as the behavioral health lead therapist at the Ruth Ellis Center for at-risk LGBT+ youth. She previously worked at the Wayne County juvenile court psychiatric clinic for 15 years, providing psychological services. Robinson earned her B.A. in psychology at Oberlin College and doctorate in clinical psychology at the University of Michigan where she has taught LGBT and multicultural courses in the Women's Studies Department. Robinson conducts cultural competence workshops and is a trainer for the Michigan Department of Education. Robinson has published articles on domestic violence in Black lesbian communities, Black lesbian youth resiliency, and Black LGBT and gender nonconforming youth in juvenile justice. Robinson coined the term "attractionality" to replace "sexuality" when referring to one's identity. She is a member of the Association of Black Psychologists and Association for Women in Psychology, having served on both boards.

Jama Shelton is an associate professor at the Silberman School of Social Work at Hunter College and the associate director of the Silberman Center for Sexuality and Gender at Hunter College. After receiving their PhD in social welfare from the Graduate Center of the City University of New York in 2013, Shelton spent 3 years working at True Colors United where they engaged in national organizing, policy, and research activities geared toward addressing LGBTQ+ youth homelessness across the country and in Europe. Shelton continues to work with True Colors United as the chief research officer, overseeing research projects in the U.S., Europe, and Central Asia in partnership with the European Federation of Organisations Working with the Homeless (FEANTSA) and the International Lesbian, Gay, Bisexual, Transgender and Intersex Association (ILGA). Shelton's research examines homelessness among LGBTQ+ youth, with particular attention to the experiences of transgender and gender expansive youth and the structural barriers rooted in cisgenderism, racism, and economic inequality that transgender and gender expansive youth face in exiting homelessness and maintaining housing stability.

WORKSHOP SPEAKERS

José Bauermeister, M.P.H., Ph.D., is the Albert M. Greenfield Professor of Human Relations at the University of Pennsylvania. Bauermeister is committed to addressing health inequities among LGBT youth of color through his scholarship. Given his expertise in applied sexuality and health research, Bauermeister co-edited the first LGBT specific book focused on health research (LGBTQ Health Research: Theory, Methods & Practice), published by the Johns Hopkins University Press and served as associate editor of the APA Handbook of Sexuality and Psychology and the SAGE Handbook of LGBT Lives in Context. Bauermeister is chair of the Department of Family and Community Health at the Penn School of Nursing, Director of the Penn Program on Sexuality, Technology & Action Research, and Professor of Psychiatry at the Perelman School of Medicine. Bauermeister is also chair of the National Institutes of Health's (NIH) Population and Public Health Approaches to HIV/AIDS Study Section, and a standing member of the NIH's Council of Councils' Sexual and Gender Minority Research Working Group. He received his bachelor's degree in psychology from the University of Puerto Rico (2002) and his master's (2004) and doctorate (2007) in public health from the University of Michigan.

Bernadette Brown, J.D., is the president of B. Brown Consulting, LLC. She provides consulting, training and technical assistance to federal, state, and local government agencies (and allied organizations) on the development, implementation, and enforcement of policies, procedures, and best practices designed to support the safety and well-being of LGBTQI+ people in detention. Some of Brown's clients include the National Institute of Corrections, U.S. Naval Consolidated Brig, Miramar, South Carolina Department of Juvenile Justice, Alameda County Probation Department (California), Maricopa County Probation Department (Arizona), Pennsylvania Bureau of Juvenile Justice Services, Michigan Center for Youth Justice, Durham Veteran Affairs Medical Center (North Carolina), and U.S. Department of Justice: Bureau of Prisons, Office of Juvenile Justice and Delinquency Prevention, and Civil Rights Division. Prior to launching B. Brown Consulting, she was the deputy legislative director at the New York Civil Liberties Union. She began her career as a public defender in New York City and has served as the director of the Center for Sexual and Gender Diversity at Duke University, and a senior program specialist at the National Council on Crime and Delinquency in California. She is also a faculty member of the National Prison Rape Elimination Act (PREA) Resource Center, where she developed the LGBTI and GNC (gender nonconforming) training curriculum for people seeking to become certified PREA auditors by the U.S. Department of Justice. She received her A.B. from Columbia University and her J.D. from Boston University School of Law.

Shelley L. Craig, Ph.D., is professor at the Factor-Inwentash Faculty of Social Work (FIFSW) at the University of Toronto and Canada Research

Chair in Sexual and Gender Minority Youth (SGMY). Drawing on 25 years of community and clinical practice, Craig's program of research is focused on: (1) understanding the experiences of SGMY in systems of care and community, (2) developing affirmative programs and interventions to cultivate SGMY resilience, (3) exploring the role of technology on SGMY well-being, and (4) enhancing equity, diversity, and inclusion in organizations. Craig has developed and tested several of the first evidence-informed interventions for SGMY mental health. She is also the principal investigator of INQYR, an international and interdisciplinary research partnership designed to train LGBTQ+ graduate students in SGMY research and conduct critical studies to support their well-being. Craig has been very involved in LGBTQ+ communities. She has served in leadership roles as founder and Executive Director of SGMY nonprofits and as Board co-chair of organizations such as WorldPride and the Council of Sexual Orientation and Gender Expression and Identity of the Council of Social Work Education (CSWE).

J. Garrett-Walker, Ph.D., is an associate professor in the Department of Applied Psychology and Human Development at the University of Toronto, Ontario Institute for Studies in Education. She earned her B.A. from University of San Francisco and her Ph.D. from the Graduate Center of City University of New York. Garrett-Walker is a developmental psychologist whose research focuses on mental health and multiple identity development for two-spirit, lesbian, gay, bisexual, transgender, and queer (2SLGBTQ+) emerging adults with a focus in Black, Indigenous, and other People of Color (BIPOC). Garrett-Walker utilizes quantitative and qualitative methodologies to examine the intersections of multiple identities; specifically gender, race, religion, and sexuality. Garrett-Walker is most interested in the ways in which BIPOC 2SLGBTQ+ young adults maintain positive mental health and well-being in the face of negative religious rhetoric, racism, homophobia, transphobia, cissexism, and heterosexism. Garrett-Walker's work has emphasized the role of identity in the development of culturally competent HIV prevention interventions and community resources. Garrett-Walker also has a line of inquiry that examines the ways in which shared educational privilege impacts color-blind racial ideologies and privilege awareness among college students. Garrett-Walker implemented a university-wide social marketing campaign at University of San Francisco, *Check Your Privilege*, that sought to raise student, faculty, and staff awareness around social inequalities and privilege. The campaign went viral on the internet and has been implemented at universities from Turtle Island to New Zealand. All of Garrett-Walker's research challenges systems and structures that seek to oppress and marginalize racialized gender and sexually expansive people. Garrett-Walker's research focuses on the ways in which BIPOC 2SLGBTQ+ people survive and thrive as opposed to the pathology entrenched in psychology.

Karina Gattamorta, Ph.D., is a research associate professor at the School of Nursing and Health Studies at the University of Miami whose work focuses on racial/ethnic sexual minority youth and their families. She has conducted research on the coming out experiences of Hispanic sexual minorities and their effects on youth and parents and has also examined health disparities of sexual minority high school students. Recently, she has examined the role of family rejection, racism, and living arrangements on psychological distress and sexual and gender minority-related stressors such as internalized homophobia, internalized transphobia, LGBTQ identity concealment, and LGBTQ victimization among LGBTQ college students. Currently, she is working on developing a measure of acceptance for parents and caregivers of LGBTQ youth and is also evaluating the feasibility and acceptability of an intervention to promote acceptance among Hispanic families. Her goals are to continue working with diverse sexual and gender minority youth and their families to help increase acceptance and reduce rejection that is linked to disparities in mental and behavioral health among this population. Gattamorta is also involved in mentoring underrepresented and minority students through her role as the program director for the Minority Health Research Training (MHRT) program at the School of Nursing and Health Studies and through mentoring programs for first-generation and LGBTQ students at the University of Miami.

Kezia Gilyard is a nonbinary educator, facilitator, and curriculum creator who uses they/them pronouns. Currently, they serve the students, employees, and families of Broward County Public Schools as the LGBTQ+ Coordinator. Their areas of specialization include facilitating conversations and building courses which allow participants to examine the experiences of students who have been marginalized by various and intersecting systems of oppression. Gilyard has trained both pre-K–12 and post-secondary educators across the country about the importance of approaching queer and trans equity through an intersectional lens. They have spent nearly a decade providing guidance, mentorship, and leadership opportunities for queer and trans youth in South Florida and beyond. Gilyard was recently selected as one of South Florida Gay News' "Out 50," a distinguished list recognizing openly LGBTQ individuals who make an impact in South Florida. Gilyard is also a recipient of the Bishop S.F. Makalani-Mahee award for Trans Equality for their work supporting transgender youth and was a finalist for GLSEN's Educator of the Year award in 2020.

Naomi Goldberg, M.P.P., is the deputy director and LGBTQ program director at the Movement Advancement Project (MAP), an independent think tank focused on providing independent and rigorous research, insight, and communications that help speed equality and opportunity for all. For more than 13 years, Goldberg has focused on advancing LGBTQ public policy with a focus on engaging, collaborative, and data-centered efforts. At MAP, she frequently collaborates with leading LGBTQ organizations and progressive allied organizations on issues including LGBTQ people and the criminal justice system, the importance of marriage for same-sex couples and their families, and the challenges facing LGBTQ workers, LGBTQ women, and LGBTQ people of color. Prior to joining MAP, Goldberg completed a public policy fellowship at the Williams Institute at UCLA School of Law. Goldberg has published in the *Archives of Sexual Behavior, Fertility and Sterility, Journal of Health Psychology* about findings from the U.S. Longitudinal Lesbian Family Study, a study of data from the California Health Interview Survey about intimate partner violence in *Journal of Interpersonal Violence,* and several book chapters about LGBTQ-parent families and economic well-being, LGBTQ family law, and transgender people and economic security. She received her master's of public policy from the University of Michigan's Ford School of Public Policy and graduated from Mount Holyoke College.

Ghirlandi Guidetti, J.D., (he/him/his) is a staff attorney in the ACLU of Illinois' LGBTQ & HIV Project where he is involved in a broad range of advocacy and litigation on behalf of LGBTQ individuals and people living with HIV. Since he joined the ACLU in the fall of 2015, Ghirlandi has focused his practice on representing youth, including students whose schools have denied them use of the facilities that match their gender identity, solely because they are transgender. He has also utilized the ACLU's long-standing consent decree with DCFS (B.H. v. Smith) to investigate the experiences of LGBTQ youth in the child welfare system and advocate for reforms to better protect and serve this vulnerable population. Ghirlandi is a graduate of Loyola University Chicago where he earned his J.D. and a master of public policy degree.

Stacey S. Horn, Ph.D., is a professor and head of the Department of Family Social Science in the College of Education and Human Development at the University of Minnesota. Her current research focuses on issues of sexual prejudice and bias-motivated harassment among adolescents and parents of adolescents, adolescents' reasoning about peer harassment, as well as LGBT students' experiences in schools and communities. Much of this work looks at the underlying moral, social, and personal dimension of exclusion and peer harassment, how adolescents construct an understanding of their peer interactions based on these dimension, and the role that bias plays in adolescents' understanding and experiences of harassment. She has published articles in journals such as *Developmental Psychology, Journal of Social Issues, Journal of Youth and Adolescence, Cognitive Development,* and *Equity and Excellence in Education*. Her edited book (with Stephen Russell) Sexual Orientation, Gender Identity, and Schooling: The Nexus of Research, Practice, and Policy won the best social policy book from SRA as well as the best book award from APA Division 44. She is a past recipient of the University Scholar award and the Award for Excellence in Teaching from UIC, as well as the Wayne F. Placek Award from the American Psychological Foundation (2002). Horn is a former high school English teacher and has worked with young people for over 30 years.

David M. Huebner, PhD, MPH, received his PhD in clinical psychology from Arizona State University and his MPH in epidemiology from the University of California, Berkeley. He is currently an associate professor in the Department of Prevention and Community Health at George Washington University (GWU), and co-director of the Social and Behavioral Sciences Core at the Washington, DC Center for AIDS Research. Prior to joining the faculty at GWU, he was on the faculty in the Department of Psychology at the University of Utah and in the School of Medicine at the Center for AIDS Prevention Studies at the University of California, San Francisco. His research examines how discrimination from families, schools, and communities impacts HIV risk and other health outcomes among sexual minority adolescents and young adults, and how preventive interventions can help mitigate those impacts. Huebner has a strong commitment to mentoring doctoral students and junior faculty, particularly those from underrepresented groups. He is also committed to supporting community organizations' efforts to engage in evidence-based practices—he has served on several local and regional HIV prevention community planning groups, and was the chair of the National Board of Directors for the Gay, Lesbian, Straight Education Network (GLSEN), a national nonprofit with a $7 million annual budget, that seeks to improve K–12 school experience for sexual and gender minority youth.

Deborah S. Levine, M.A., M.S.W., is the director of LGBT YouthLink, a division of CenterLink. She has been championing for the health needs of adolescents for the plurality of her career, working for a decade as the Director of Online Health Education at Planned Parenthood. Prior to that, she worked at a local Planned Parenthood providing career development training for youth serving professionals and managing a peer education program. Her insight into the experiences of youth is furthered by her background in education; she taught American history at Boston area public high schools. She is the founder and operator of Q Chat Space, an online LGBTQ+ space where teens can join live, chat-based, professionally facilitated support groups. As such, Levine is highly familiar with both the health needs of sexual and gender minority youth and the ability of digital technology to help in meeting those needs in highly innovative ways. In her current role at YouthLink, Levine not only oversees Q Chat Space but also supports the development of youth programs at LGBT community centers across the country through networking opportunities for program staff, peer-based technical assistance and training, and a variety of capacity building services.

Malcolm Lin is a junior at the University of Kansas studying in the social welfare field. They spent 4 years as part of a youth advisory board for research. They are looking to do research in the social welfare field after they graduate with a bachelor's degree. Lin did research in transgender and gender diverse youth diversity. They worked with several transgender youths and talked about the different issues they went through. The group they worked with included primarily Caucasians, while they themselves were one of two persons of color on the youth advisory board. They brought in many different perspectives on being transgender and a person of color.

Alison Macklin, MSW, is a national leader in the comprehensive sex education field for over 17 years. In 2019, she helped author and pass Colorado's Youth Wellness Act, ensuring young people in that state are able to access inclusive comprehensive sex education. As senior policy advisor for SIECUS: Sex Ed for Social Change, she provides strategic guidance to communities looking to advance comprehensive sex education at the state and federal level. Macklin is the author of the internationally published book: "Making Sense of It: A Guide to Sex for Teens (and Their Parents Too!)," and a skilled sex education trainer with a Masters of Social Work degree from University of Denver.

Allen Mallory is a presidential postdoctoral scholar at The Ohio State University in the Department of Human Sciences. He received his Ph.D. from the University of Texas at Austin in Human Development and Family Sciences where he was also a trainee at the University of Texas Population Research Center. Mallory's research takes an intersectional approach in understanding the health and well-being of sexual and gender minorities. Specifically, he studies how health disparities vary among and between sexual and gender minorities across multiple marginalized identities and how the processes tied to multiple identities, such as discrimination, intersect to affect the health of youth and adults. Mallory was funded by an F31 to investigate how race, gender, and sexual identity discrimination were independent and overlapping in their prospective associations with mental health. He was recently awarded an NIH Loan Repayment Program through NIDA where he will examine variability in the treatment effects of substance use interventions by sexual identity.

Sarah Mountz, Ph.D., is an assistant professor at University at Albany School of Social Welfare. Her research, teaching, and practice focus on the experiences of LGBTQ+ youth in child welfare and juvenile justice systems using an intersectional lens. She utilizes participatory approaches and arts-based and other qualitative methods in her work to center and amplify youth voice and promote critical consciousness and youth activism. Mountz practiced as a social worker in the child welfare system in New York City prior to pursuing her doctorate in social welfare from the University of Washington. Her work has been featured in several peer-reviewed journals and books, including *Child Welfare, Affilia, Children and Youth Services Review, the Journal of Public Child Welfare, the Journal of the Society of Social Work and Research, the Sage Encyclopedia of LGBTQ Studies*, and *Case Studies for Affirmative Social Work Practice with LGBTQ+ Individuals and Communities*. Mountz teaches, trains, and consults on issues pertaining to systems impacted youth and families and the intersections of race, gender/gender identity, sexual orientation, and other axes of identity.

John Pachankis, Ph.D., is the Susan Dwight Bliss Associate Professor of Public Health and Psychiatry at Yale. As director of Yale's LGBTQ Mental Health Initiative, his goal is to bring effective mental health treatments to LGBTQ people in the United States and around the world and to identify strategies to getting such treatment to LGBTQ people in greatest need. His NIH-funded studies examine the efficacy of LGBTQ-affirmative interventions delivered via diverse technologies, settings, and community members. These interventions have shown efficacy for reducing the co-occurring mental health risks commonly affecting LGBTQ people (e.g., depression, anxiety, suicidality, substance use disorders) across several randomized controlled trials. He has published 100+ scientific papers on LGBTQ mental health and stigma and co-edited the *Handbook of Evidence-Based Mental Health Practice with Sexual and Gender Minorities* published by Oxford University Press and has received several awards for his research, including APA's Distinguished Contribution to Psychology in the Public Interest award, Distinguished Contribution to the Advancement of Psychotherapy award, and awards for Distinguished Book and Distinguished Scientific Contribution to LGBTQ scholarship.

Paul Poteat, Ph.D., is professor in the Department of Counseling, Developmental, and Educational Psychology at Boston College. His research focuses on the school-based experiences of sexual and gender minority youth. With support from NIH and IES, his research on Gender-Sexuality Alliances (GSAs) has identified individual- and group-level mechanisms by which these school-based clubs promote empowerment and resilience among youth from diverse sexual orientations and gender identities. His work also examines bias-based harassment using an ecological framework to identify individual and peer factors that contribute to such behavior or that buffer against its effects. Poteat has served as an associate editor for the *Journal of Research on Adolescence,* the *American Educational Research Journal,* and *The Counseling Psychologist,* and is the current co-chair of the Equity and Justice Committee of the Society for Research in Child Development.

Myeshia Price, Ph.D. (she/they), is a senior research scientist at The Trevor Project. Price has more than 15 years of experience in adolescent public health research, with a focus on sexuality, gender, and LGBTQ youth from an intersectional perspective. After completing their Ph.D. in developmental psychology at the University of Wisconsin-Madison with research focusing on predicting early sexual behaviors during adolescence, they were an assistant professor at the State University of New York at Old Westbury prior to taking a research position at the Center for Innovative Public Health Research (CiPHR). Her primary research interest areas include developmental understandings of adolescent gender and sexuality and reducing LGBTQ youth mental health disparities with a particular focus on the role of protective factors.

Lilianna Angel Reyes, M.P.A., a trans Latina woman and graduate from the University of Michigan school system, has extensive history in leading organizations and coalitions focused on reducing social and health disparities of marginalized populations. She has worked with many state and national civil rights organizations, and government and corporate entities such as Planned Parenthood, Detroit Police LGBT Advisory Council, Michigan Department of Health and Human Services, and many others. Reyes is a longtime member of the Iconic House of Ebony, now serving as the Detroit Godmother for the house and was recently inducted in the Detroit Ballroom Hall of Fame 2020. Reyes most recently spoke at the United Nations on the status of trans women of color in the global call for women's success. Currently, she serves as Youth Drop-In Director at the Ruth Ellis Center, and is also the executive director of a transformative Detroit based nonprofit, The Trans Sistas of Color Project (TSOCP). Under her leadership, the organization won the Detroit Spirit Award 2020. Reyes was highlighted in USA Today's Faces of Pride 2017, 100 Women of the Century 2020, and in NBC's OUT Pride List 2020, Google's Pride Spaces 2021, Adidas dedication to Ballroom 2021, and USA Today Pride 2021 campaign.

Benita Ramsey, J.D., is a justice and culture strategist and practitioner, a spiritual director, and a lover of books, words, rhythms, and beats. A gifted Spoken Word artist and wordsmith, Ramsey is a third-generation Pentecostal style storyteller and preacher. She serves as a program support manager for the Inland Empire HIV Planning Council and executive director of Rainbow Pride Youth Alliance. She is a principal consultant for BRMG Management Group specializing in social justice, diversity, and inclusion. Ramsey serves as a community consultant to Riverside University Health System Behavioral Health, Lesbian Gay Bisexual Transgender Outreach Initiatives. She currently serves on the advisory board for We BREATHE, the Statewide LGBTQ Tobacco Control Project and on the Steering Committee for the CA LGBTQ Health and Human Services Network. Ramsey is an ordained minister and pastor at Unity Fellowship Church-IE, a former College Dean of Students at the Claremont Colleges, and an ethnic services manager. Ramsey received her master's degree in African American Studies and Women's History from the University of Wisconsin–Madison and a Juris Doctorate from the University of Miami School of Law.

Margaret Rosario, PhD., is a professor of psychology at The City University of New York. Her research focuses on identity and stress, as well as the implications of each for health and other adaptive outcomes. The research has primarily centered on lesbian, gay, and bisexual young people undergoing sexual identity development. In addition, she is interested in the determinants of sexual orientation and the intersection of multiple identities. Rosario is the recipient of research grants. She is a Fellow of the American Psychological Association and the Society for the Scientific Study of Sexuality. She is an associate editor of the *Journal of Sex Research* and a member of several editorial boards. She is past president of Division 44 of the American Psychological Association, the Society for the Psychology of Sexual Orientation and Gender Diversity. Rosario did her postdoctoral training at Columbia University's College of Physicians and Surgeons, her doctorate at New York University, and her bachelor's degree at Princeton University.

Renata Sanders, M.D., M.P.H., S.C.M., is an associate professor of adolescent medicine, pediatrics and internal medicine at Johns Hopkins University School of Medicine. Her areas of clinical expertise include adolescent sexually transmitted infection and HIV, adolescent transition to adult care, caring for sexual and gender minority youth, and school-based health center needs. She serves as the medical director of the Pediatric and Adolescent HIV/AIDS Program, director of the PrEP Program (prepisforyouth.org), co-director of the Emerge Gender and Sexuality Clinic, and the co-director of the Adolescent and Young Adult Scientific Working Group, Johns Hopkins Center for AIDS Research. She has served as a consultant to the Centers for Disease Control and Prevention to make recommendations regarding

HIV testing laws in Maryland and has worked locally with the Baltimore City Health Department to improve HIV testing strategies in youth aged 15 to 24.

Sanders's leadership achievements have been recognized in multiple awards and roles in committees nationally and across the institution. In 2007, she was selected out of 300 applicants to attend the National Institute of Child Health & Human Development Summer Institute in Applied Research on Child and Adolescent Development. She has been selected to participate in two career development programs for women faculty—the Association of American Medical Colleges Early Career Women Faculty Professional Development Seminar and the 2015 Johns Hopkins School of Medicine Leadership Program for Women Faculty.

Carlos E. Santos, Ph.D., is an associate professor in the Luskin School of Public Affairs' Department of Social Welfare at the University of California, Los Angeles. His research is focused on studying ethnic-racial identity, gender identity, and sexual minority identity using an intersectional approach. He employs developmental theories and empirical methodologies in order to study the contexts within which identities are formed, develop, and change over time among primarily Latinx youth. He has been recognized for "pioneering" research that shows the effect of peer networks on identity formation, and was awarded multiple early career awards for achievement in research from three different national professional associations. His research has been funded by both the National Science Foundation and National Institutes of Health, and he is a member of the National Academy of Sciences' Forum on Children's Well-Being.

Russell Toomey, Ph.D., is Program Chair and Professor of Family Studies and Human Development at the University of Arizona. He also serves as the interim director of the Institute for LGBT Studies at the University of Arizona. He conducts research on the processes by which sexual and gender minority youth thrive and are resilient despite the oppressive barriers and challenges they encounter in society. Toomey's research identifies both the individual-level mechanisms (e.g., coping, activism) and systems-level policies (e.g., inclusive school policies) that reduce the impacts of discrimination and contribute to optimal health, well-being, and educational outcomes. At the University of Arizona, he teaches undergraduate and graduate courses on adolescent development, human sexuality, and advanced graduate-level applied statistics. He serves on the Executive Council for the Society for Research on Adolescence.

Manal Vishnoi is an incoming sophomore at UC San Diego majoring in chemistry. They are also an intern with the Youth Services' Pride Youth

Program in Glenview, and have been involved in LGBTQ+ youth work since middle school. They were the GSA (Gay-Straight Alliance) leader for 2 years at Deerfield High School. They fought to change many issues at their high school to help make life better for LGBTQ+ students.

Angela Weeks, D.B.A., brings extensive national experience creating, implementing, and evaluating programs and initiatives that improve the lives of LGBTQ+ people and communities. Weeks is the project director for The National Quality Improvement Center on Tailored Services, Placement Stability, and Permanency for LGBTQ2S Children and Youth in Foster Care (QIC-LGBTQ2S). As the project director for the QIC-LGBTQ2S, she has helped develop, implement, and evaluate 15 different LGBTQ+ programs and initiatives for LGBTQ+ foster youth, their families, and the workforce that serves them. She also has extensive experience supporting LGBTQ+ populations experiencing homelessness and the juvenile justice system and leads the Center of Excellence on LGBTQ+ Behavioral Health Equity.

Bianca D.M. Wilson, Ph.D., is the Rabbi Zacky Senior Scholar of Public Policy at the Williams Institute. Her research focuses primarily on system-involved LGBTQ youth, LGBT poverty, and sexual health among queer women. In addition to multiple peer-reviewed and institution-published reports, she co-edited a special issue of the *Journal of Lesbian Studies* that featured a multidisciplinary collection of work on health and other topics from the perspectives of Black lesbians in the U.S., Caribbean, and South Africa. She earned a doctorate in psychology from the Community and Prevention Research program at the University of Illinois at Chicago with a minor in statistics, methods, and measurement, and received postdoctoral training at the University of California, San Francisco (UCSF) Institute for Health Policy Studies and the UCSF Lesbian Health and Research Center through an Agency for Health Research and Quality postdoctoral fellowship.

Geoffrey Winder is an LGBTQ+ youth advocate with over 20 years of experience. He is currently co-executive director of Genders & Sexualities Alliance (GSA) Network, a national organization supporting LGBTQ youth through GSA clubs across the country. He was formerly a GSA club youth leader at his own high school as well as a GSA Network alumni. Winder joined GSA Network's full-time staff in 2008. Prior to becoming co-executive director in 2015, he led GSA Network's Racial and Economic Justice programs for 5 years, and emerged as a national leader on LGBTQ youth and education justice issues. This work focused on understanding the impacts of the "School-to-Prison Pipeline" on LGBTQ youth of color, and organizing to address policies, practices, and patterns that disproportionately impact LGBTQ youths' access to a quality education. In his current role he continues to ensure the organization's analyses, programs and culture meet the needs of the most vulnerable LGBTQ student populations. He holds a B.A. in Change Theory and Globalization from New York University's Gallatin School for Individualized Study.